Successful and Sustainable Data Policies

A Guide for Enabling Data Governance at Scale

Malcolm Chisholm Ph.D.

Technics Publications

SEDONA, ARIZONA

TECHNICS PUBLICATIONS

TECHNOLOGY / LEADERSHIP

115 Linda Vista, Sedona, AZ 86336 USA

https://www.TechnicsPub.com

Edited by Jamie Hoberman

Cover design by Lorena Molinari

First Printing 2024

Copyright © 2024 by Malcolm Chisholm Ph.D.

ISBN, print ed.	9781634626095
ISBN, Kindle ed.	9781634626101
ISBN, PDF ed.	9781634626118

Library of Congress Control Number: 2024951365

When a country is rebellious, it has many rulers,
but a ruler with discernment and knowledge maintains order.
-Proverbs 28:2 (NIV)

Acknowledgments

I owe a great debt of gratitude to those I have worked with and who helped me to understand the subject matter of policies, especially Susan Garza. The production of this book would not have been possible without the patience of my family, especially my wife Rina. Additionally, I would like to thank Carla Guerrero for all the planning, coordination, and attention to detail she provided throughout the entire process.

Contents

Figures

Tables

## Chapter 1

Introduction

We often hear that data is the fuel of the Information Age and the most important resource in modern economies. If that is the case, then common sense tells us that we should manage data carefully, just as we do for other valuable and important resources.

The reality is that data is not managed as well as it should be.

We can easily find examples of poor data quality, duplicate copies of data that incrementally add to storage costs, data that is not correctly understood and interpreted, personal data that is mishandled, and so on.

In part, this seems to be due to an expectation that the technology housing and processing data will deal with all these management needs. But humans interact with data frequently. We get to decide what data goes into computerized systems, what the data means, how it is input, how it is processed, how it needs to be secured, what we do with the outputs of these systems, how data is eventually disposed of, and many other tasks. In other words, there is a great deal of primarily human behavior around data that is only indirectly related to technology.

Perhaps we may not be concerned about these behaviors in our private lives, but in the organizations we work for it is a different matter. All modern enterprises are highly reliant on data, and staff in one part of an organization are often reliant on data from another part. This complexity increases the need for good data management by all staff interacting with the data.

This is where data policies come in. Data policies seek to improve human behaviors around data in organizations to reach a reasonable level of good data management practices. This cannot be done with technology alone because some human interactions are never going to be replaced by automation. People are always going to interact with data.

Where We Are Today

Without data policies, staff manage data only if they realize they need to, and in *ad hoc* ways that vary widely. Perhaps some of these practices are good, but often they are not, and many times required practices are simply absent. This is not to blame anyone; it is just the way things have evolved.

Over the past two decades, executive management has come to realize the value of data, and that there are significant problems with extracting value from that data. New technologies like AI are providing the means to extract that value, but the "data messes" in most organizations prevent the desired realization of business benefit. As a result, executives have invested resources and authority in Data Governance units that are charged with solving the "data messes." Data policies are expected to be part of the solution.

As if this was not enough, the need to reduce risk in data has become increasingly apparent. Many events, like the 2008 Global Financial Crisis and the introduction of data privacy laws, have also impacted executive thinking. The result is that Data Governance units are expected to introduce data policies to deal with specific data-related risks.

The Purpose of This Book

It is, therefore, a given today that effective data policies are needed. How is this to be achieved? Data Governance units are staffed with experts in specialized aspects of data, but they do not necessarily understand how to develop, operationalize, and maintain successful and sustainable data policies. A Data Governance unit probably has the knowledge to write a number of data policies. Still, there is a huge gap between that and getting the policies adhered to across an entire enterprise, and producing the intended outcomes.

This book seeks to provide detailed and practical guidance on how make data policies work. As the title suggests, there are two basic concepts involved, which are:

- "Successful" meaning having a portfolio of operationalized data policies that ensure human data management practices lead to the required level of value realization and risk management for the enterprise's data resource as a whole. Data policies that do not contribute to these goals are not put in place.

- "Sustainable" meaning that the data policies stay in force and relevant over time. As needs arise, new data policies are introduced, existing ones are updated, and policies no longer needed are discontinued. The mechanisms by which this administration is performed run continuously.

The philosophy of this book is that institutionalization is necessary to have successful and sustainable data policies.

Institutionalization means building a set of practices for decision-making and administration of data policies without any reliance on specific people. An organizational framework ensures data policies of the highest quality are produced and adhered to across the enterprise.

The book focuses on the policy lifecycle as a way of decomposing the work needed for data policies into manageable chunks for which the required institutional capacity can be built one piece at a time. The individual phases of the policy lifecycle are all quite different, and it is not possible to think of "data policies" as a simple whole without this detailed breakdown.

Why Institutionalization?

Let's explore why we need an institutional approach to data policies in more detail.

If we think about governance in general, what is the alternative to an ordered institutionalized system?

Most probably it would be autocracy, which for data policies would likely mean the head of Data Governance making all the important decisions by themselves or in consultation with whomever they like. Alternatively, the head of Data Governance may just tell an analyst to do the work. Thus, data policies become highly dependent on individuals. If the head of Data Governance changes, the next head may not see the importance of data policies at all and stop supporting them. Or they may dislike the current policies and seek to replace them. It is also possible that the head of Data Governance, or the analyst they designate, may not be good at drafting policies. Too much goes wrong when things depend on particular people without any institutional framework.

One way around this is to try to formalize "roles and responsibilities." For instance, an analyst can have writing data policies as part of their job description. The analyst can even be given the role name "Data Policy Analyst." This goes well with the managerial philosophy of making one person responsible for something and holding them accountable. However, this too is nothing more than an individual task assignment, albeit more formalized. The analyst can have their responsibilities changed at a moment's notice. A reorganization, such as frequently happens when leadership changes, can do away with the role of "Data Policy Analyst." The individual can leave the organization, taking their knowledge with them, and finding a replacement "Data Policy Analyst" may not be possible.

Institutionalization means turning over the decision-making framework for arriving at data policies to organizational structures with broad participation, rather than assigning decisions to particular individuals. It also includes establishing sound administrative practices directed by these organizational structures to ensure the policies are managed, operationalized, and evaluated effectively. The result is an unstoppable organizational "machine" for data policies whose enormous momentum ensures the production of data policies of the highest quality, and enforces compliance with them.

Good Governance and Institutionalization

There is another line of reasoning for why institutionalizing data policies is needed. Policies are the most powerful tool a Data Governance unit has. A Data Governance unit staffed by a handful of people can produce significant changes in business behaviors across an entire enterprise by issuing data policies.

This level of power has to be exercised with extreme caution. Data policies cannot be the result of point-in-time decisions taken alone by particular individuals. If this is done, the data policies produced will likely be disruptive rather than helpful. Unfortunately, such problems often occur, and when they do, executive management may remove policy authority from a Data Governance unit and give it to another area like Risk or Legal. In some cases, the Data Governance unit may even be disbanded.

Good governance means that decision-making frameworks must exist that have broad participation and foster collaboration. This requires building institutional bodies to deal with data policies. Autocracy is simply not good governance.

At this point, we frequently hear the objection that this is bureaucracy. "Bureaucracy" can be an excuse for Data Governance leadership not to give up power. It can also be invoked because leadership does not know how to build effective institutional capacity for data policies. Of course, poorly designed institutionalized practices can be bureaucratic, but avoiding that outcome is one of the goals of this book.

Ceding power should not be seen as a negative, since the benefit to the enterprise greatly outweighs it. Policies are such powerful tools that they require the good governance institutionalization brings.

Why a Policy Lifecycle?

I have worked as a consultant in data governance and data management for many years and have often been asked to develop specific data policies for various needs. When I did so, I naturally thought the policies I wrote were really good. After the policies were duly handed over to my sponsors, I noticed something strange. The data policies were put in a storage location and nothing more happened. Very often the Data Governance unit involved would say that it "had" data policies, and indeed it did. But nobody else knew about them and certainly did not adhere to them. It was as if the policy artifact was an end in itself.

This was when I realized that Data Governance units were missing the many remaining steps in the policy lifecycle. Data Governance could only understand writing the policies and nothing more. Perhaps they thought staff from across the enterprise could discover the data policies, read them, and follow them without any additional effort by Data Governance. Of course, this never happened.

Getting from a draft data policy to compliance across an entire enterprise requires a complex set of procedures, and also involves technology support.

Without a well-defined policy lifecycle, Data Governance units will never understand the institutional capacity that has to be built to have successful and sustainable data policies. That is why we will focus a great deal on the policy lifecycle in this book.

Audience

This book is intended for anyone who works with data and has an interest in data policies. For a lot of the book, we will be looking at data policies from the perspective of a Data Governance unit because Data Governance is currently the main unit that manages these policies.

However, the book will also be useful in other areas. For instance, a Risk Department that is looking at data policies in general, or a Data Engineering unit that needs some specific technical data policies, will find the guidance presented here useful. Some roles in Information Technology departments, like Business Analysts, Technical Data Analysts, and Project Managers can also benefit from a deeper appreciation of data policies.

The book also applies to the areas of Analytics Governance (including Data Science) and AI Governance, which are closely related to and overlap with data governance and data management.

Conventions Used in This Book

The following conventions are used in this book:

- "Data Governance" in title case refers to an organizational unit, while "data governance" in lowercase refers to the general practice area.

- Specialized terms appear in title case so they can be understood as a complete term. For instance, "...and the Data Policy Oversight Committee does this work...," where "Data Policy Oversight Committee" is a specialized term. However, we keep the phases of the policy lifecycle in lowercase as they appear so frequently.

- Sometimes "data policies" is shortened to "policies" for brevity.

- There is a glossary of all specialized terms with their definitions.

The book begins with several foundational chapters, including a deeper rationale for needing data policies. It then defines the policy lifecycle and goes through it step by step. Matter specific to a particular phase of a policy lifecycle is dealt with in the chapter dealing with that phase. However, some of this matter is foundational and relates back to the chapter on the policy of policies.

There is much more that could be written about data policies, but the scope of this book is not intended to fully exhaust the topic, which would be impossible in any case. The book aims to provide guidance on establishing at least the foundation for successful and sustainable data policies.

## Chapter 2

What are Policies?

In order to work with data policies, we need to understand the concept of policies. Just what is a policy? It might seem to be an unnecessary question as everyone knows, but is this really so? Let's begin by exploring where policies fit into a bigger picture, then look at policies in detail, and finally consider what policies are not.

Directives

Policies exist within a wider framework of concepts, which consists of:
- Principles
- Policies
- Standards
- Practices
- Procedures

We will call them collectively "directives," and we will define the directives that apply to data as follows:

A data directive is defined as:
anything approved by the enterprise that tells staff
what data management to do, or how to do manage
data.

The enterprise is an organization like a company or unit of government that has some degree of autonomy within a legal framework to decide how it will conduct its business. It can set its own directives.

Specifications and requirements are excluded from directives as they are specific to the building phases of particular solutions. Rules are important, but in the context of data management, they are too atomic to be considered directives. They may be components of practices and procedures.

To understand policies, we have to understand how they are distinct from the other types of directives, and we will do that now.

Directive Definitions

The conceptual framework within which directives exist and the main distinctions between different types of directives are illustrated in Figure 2.1.

Figure 2.1: Directives Conceptual Framework

The definitions for the concepts in Figure 2.1 are listed below in Table 2.1.

Term	Definition
Level 1	
Vision	A description of the ideal state
Mission	How we get to the ideal state
Level 2: High-Level Planning	
Strategy	A plan that is broad in scope (perhaps enterprise-wide), longer term, and intended to help achieve the vision.
Tactic	A plan for a single step or task or some other part of a Strategy
Level 3: High-Level Planning Components	
Goal	An outcome, usually in the long term, that supports a vision and/or mission

Term	Definition
Critical Success Factor (CSF)	Something that has to be in place for the goals to be attained.
Objective	Something measurable, usually an output of an activity, that helps to achieve a goal.
Success Criteria	The specific measures by which attaining an objective is assessed.
Level 4: Directives	
Principle	A statement of fundamental belief that cannot be further analyzed, and must be accepted as true or false. Principles are used to guide actions where there are no precise policies, standards, or lower-level rules.
Policy	A high-level imperative that controls business behavior. It supports one or more principles. A policy specifies what to do but not how to do it. A policy is enforceable and enforced.
Practice	A repeatable way to implement part of a policy and/or achieve an objective.
Standard	A practice that is mandated.
Procedure	A set of instructions for performing a task in a logical sequence.

Table 2.1: Definitions of Concepts Related to Directives

Policies

Our definition of policy contains several key points:

1. A policy is an imperative – a command – that tells people to do something. This does not mean it is written in harsh language, but it must be followed.

2. A policy controls business behavior. That is, enterprise staff will have to have to do something to be in compliance with the policy. Automation may be involved, but the human element is primary.

3. A policy is aligned to principles. Principles are logically prior to policies (although we will deal with them in a later chapter). If we have a policy that does not align with any of our stated principles, then we have *de facto* principles that we are not articulating, but upon which the policy is based. If we have principles that are not related to any policies, then we may suspect that we are not really serious about these principles (although some principles may genuinely have no policies related to them).

4. A policy must not tell people how to do something. It cannot anticipate every situation and circumstance. Instead, it must specify what must be done and leave it up to the readers to figure out how to implement the policy. It is possible to specify courses of action, but these are practices, standards, and procedures.

5. A policy is enforceable. It is not a theoretical document that is put somewhere for people to read if they happen to be interested. It is not a set of suggestions. Moreover, there is a mechanism by which the policy can be enforced, and this mechanism is put in place before the policy is released to the enterprise.

6. A policy is enforced. That is, the mechanism that could be used for enforcement actually is used for

enforcement. This point is often underappreciated. Enforcement requires action. People who just want to write a policy and be done with it have to realize that they will participate in enforcement. Enforcement does not usually mean punishment (though it sometimes may). Rather, it is detecting out-of-compliance conditions and then working with the areas where these are found to fix the problem. To some extent, it is more like providing support—except the context is a mandatory one. Any support requires resources, and the Data Governance units issuing data policies must ensure they have the necessary resources to support their policies.

Policies vs. Policy Statements

A policy must have a specific and coherent scope. It cannot be a jumble of different imperatives about unrelated topics. This is pretty well understood and is usually not a problem.

By contrast, the difference between a policy and a policy statement is often less appreciated. A policy is the whole document, but a policy statement is an individual imperative located within the document.

> *Too many policies are written as huge "blobs" of text in which it is not possible to determine where one policy statement ends and another begins.*

Worse still, a policy statement may be scattered as individual sentences among other sentences that have nothing to do with the particular policy statement. We shall return to these issues later.

What a Data Policy Is Not

A data policy must not be any of the following:

- **Educational Material:** A policy does not seek to educate, that is, explain the concepts involved. Of course, data governance and data management are complex areas and some kind of education may be required for staff to understand a data policy. But this education must not be part of the data policy. There is nothing imperative in education and it will confuse the reader if it is included in the policy.

  An explanation of a policy statement is permissible within a policy to provide clarification.

  Data Governance units must consider if the target audience of a policy has the educational prerequisites to understand the policy. That is a different matter to the data policy itself and must be handled by activities like Data Literacy programs.

- **Training:** This, too, cannot be part of a data policy. It will be too much like a procedure and appear to prescribe how to implement the policy.

- **Guidelines:** These are optional advice. Policies are not optional.

- **Best Practices:** These are lessons from outside the enterprise that have been documented as successful. Despite this, they are often not specific enough for a particular organization. Some people like to try to identify them and adopt them so they do not have to do much thinking. But they are not policies.

Problems with the Word "Policy"

Words, or more properly, "terms" (including groups of words), are labels that signify concepts. A concept is a coherent idea that can be formulated as a clear and distinct definition. Terms are symbols, meaning that there is a general convention that the term signifies the concept. In everyday language, the general convention is what the popular culture normally accepts it as being. But in science, technology, law, and similar specialized fields, the convention is established formally within the particular field of endeavor.

Unfortunately, data governance is not a disciplined field of endeavor like, say, genetics, so no authoritative body, or recognized scholars, have defined its specialized terms. Furthermore, terms get hijacked in the wider field of computerization because it is so heavily commercialized. This includes data and data governance technologies, where vendors naturally face tremendous marketing pressures to use data governance terms. That is, the terms are used to hype whatever is being sold. The term "policy" gets caught up in this.

There is a more general problem in that people tend to use incorrect terms to boost less prestigious concepts to give the impression that they have a higher standing than is merited. For instance, people use terms like "iconic" and "legendary" to describe things that have no icons or legends associated with them

With "policy," we see a very striking example of such "boosting" within IT in the areas that deal with access control. Here, "policy" means a low-level, specific rule for permitting access. As we have seen, policies are not detailed rules. The unfortunate result is that when IT professionals and Data Governance professionals discuss policies, they typically mean very different things and the conversations can be incredibly confusing.

At a much higher level, we see misuse of "policy" by governments and the media that report on government activities. Governments certainly have policies in the same sense we use in this book. However, in recent years, governments have tended to use the term "policy" to mean "central planning." Because this use of the word "policy" is amplified by mainstream media, many people are familiar with it, which drives confusion when people have to deal with real policies. Figure 2.2 provides an example.

Therefore, we must be very careful to stick to the definition we have given "policy" in this chapter and make sure that everyone who has to comply with data policies understands what we mean by a "policy." Ideally, staff will understand the entire framework of directives, as shown in Figure 2.1.

One way to achieve this outcome is to include some material about data policies in Data Literacy training. Data Literacy is outside the scope of this book, but it seeks to build individual capacity in enterprise staff so that they can understand and work better with data.

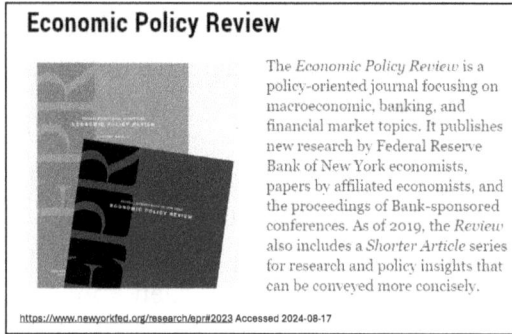

Economic Policy Review

The *Economic Policy Review* is a policy-oriented journal focusing on macroeconomic, banking, and financial market topics. It publishes new research by Federal Reserve Bank of New York economists, papers by affiliated economists, and the proceedings of Bank-sponsored conferences. As of 2019, the *Review* also includes a *Shorter Article* series for research and policy insights that can be conveyed more concisely.

https://www.newyorkfed.org/research/epr#2023 Accessed 2024-08-17

Figure 2.2: Example of The Word "Policy" Used in Central Planning

Relationships of Policies, Standards, Practices, and Procedures

As shown in Figure 2.1, there are relationships between policies, standards, practices, and procedures. Policies can beget standards and practices that help with policy operationalization, and standards and practices can lead to more detailed procedures. Furthermore, some standards, practices, and procedures can be developed at a local level, rather than an enterprise level. Not all policies have to lead to these other directives, as many policies are aimed at directly constraining human behavior around data. There is also a difference in the art of developing and implementing standards, practices, and procedures compared to policies, which we cannot cover in this book. Therefore, in the subsequent chapters, we will focus on data policies rather than their related directives.

## Chapter 3

A Brief History of Data

I f we are to develop policies for data, we ought to understand why we need to do this work. What is special about data and its role in the modern world that requires us to have policies for it?

The first point is to realize that while data cannot be entirely separated from the technology that stores and processes it, it cannot be reduced to technology, either. This is vital to grasp, and unfortunately, many people really do think that data is nothing more than technology, and that technology is the only thing we need to be concerned about. If that were true, we would only need policies for technology that would automatically cover everything required for data.

But this is not the case.

Think of technology as pipes and the data as what flows through the pipes, or technology might be like a piano, and data the music it produces.

How Did We Get Here?

To understand what is special about data and how data is bound to technology yet distinct from it, we need to understand how we got to where we are today.

If we could travel back to the early 1960s, we would notice that most normal business operations had their information recorded on paper by human clerks. If you deposited $5 in your bank account, you would have to go to a branch of the bank, hand over the cash, and a clerk would write an entry in a paper-based ledger book to record the transaction.

That was how bookkeeping was done to capture the information about the operational transactions of enterprises. It had been done that way for hundreds, probably thousands, of years, with innovation and improvement over time.

The Mainframe Revolution

Beginning in 1965, mainframe computers became available to businesses of all sizes. These computers could be purchased or licensed. Perhaps more significantly, computers could be rented on demand to do processing (known as "time-sharing"), which meant that even relatively small organizations could access them cost-effectively.

The first thing that happened was that businesses began to automate the bookkeeping activities that had been done by clerical staff up to that point. Of course, humans were still needed to enter data, run the computers, and take actions based on outputs provided by the computers. More importantly, humans were also needed to program the computers so the computers could process the operational information fed into them.

Figure 3.1: An IBM Mainframe in the 1970's

Nevertheless, businesses gained considerable advantages from this revolution, including those shown in Table 3.1.

#	Benefits of Automating Manual Bookkeeping Processes
1	Automated data processing replaced human clerks processing information. The processing had to be programmed once but could be run an indefinite number of times, unlike previously when people did all the processing.
2	Much easier and cheaper copying of information, including safeguarding it via backups.
3	Business operations could be scaled more easily because there was no need to add more clerical staff as this happened.
4	Greater reliability of processing as computers always ran the same processing instructions they were initially programmed with. People could make "bookkeeping errors."

Table 3.1: Advantages of Automating Manual Bookkeeping Processes

As for the data, it was conceptually the same as it was during the era of manual processing. The only difference now was that it was held in electronic and not paper form, and the processing was automated. The inputs to and outputs from the automated processes typically remained in terms of content, although the formats changed.

Data was not thought of much in its own right but was usually considered just to be a byproduct of data processing.

Complexity and the Rise of Databases

Automating simple standalone bookkeeping processes was so successful that more complex processes became candidates for automation.

For instance, the US securities industry ("Wall Street") suffered from what was called the "Backoffice Crisis" in the late 1970's. All processes were hitherto manual, but the number of daily transactions grew to a point where manual processes were overwhelmed and the stock exchanges could not function properly. The solution was rapid automation. However, this involved many interrelated processes, like order capture, trade authorization, balance checks, trade matching, settlement, delivery, and so on.

The automation of separate processes with many different datasets that were somehow related was one of the drivers towards databases. A database is a data storage platform where different datasets are related together. Figure 3.2

illustrates this concept. As the 1970s rolled by, databases gradually rose to prominence, and this presented problems.

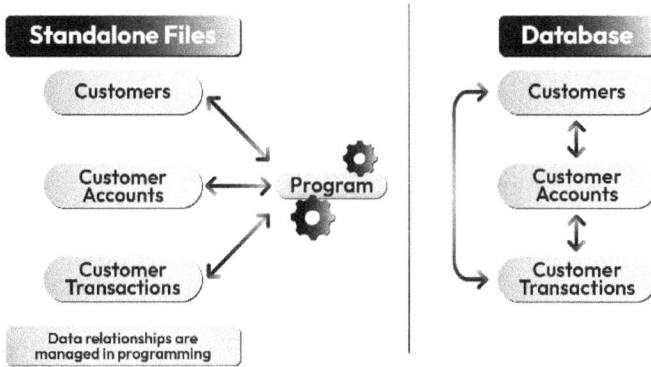

Figure 3.2: Database versus Standalone Files

With simple bookkeeping processes, there was often just a single dataset, usually called a file. The specification was exactly what was used in the bookkeeping process. But databases had to be designed, and designed well because they were shared among many processes. No one process could simply dictate the database design. Design errors in databases were found to cause significant errors in processes. For the first time, data got noticed and people started to think it might be important.

Relational Databases and Data Modeling

In 1970, E. F. Codd published a set of rules for how data should be organized in relational databases, called "Normalization." Relational databases are one type of database architecture. Initially, there were other kinds of databases, but over the years the relational model came to dominate. Codd provided something not seen before – a theory and practice for designing data stores to minimize update errors. Data had started to become a thing in its own right.

Later, in 1976, Peter Chen developed a notation that could be used to visualize database designs, including some of the rules that Codd had formulated. This opened up the possibility of developing visual blueprints for a database – a practice known as Data Modeling. Eventually, Data Modeling tools arose that made the practice even more mainstream. Again, something had been developed purely for data rather than the technology that processed it.

The Rise and First Fall of IT Departments

After the start of the computer revolution in 1965, Information Technology (IT) departments began to grow and become very large. They were known by other names at various points in time, but we will stick with "IT."

IT departments did a good job, but there were issues under the surface. The people who worked in them usually knew little of the business of the organization in which the IT department was located. In fact, IT staff were often more oriented to the IT industry than their parent organizations. IT departments were always cost centers – they consumed money without directly producing revenue. Executives naturally disliked this. Over time, IT departments have consistently pushed to acquire more and more of the latest technology. As executives frequently had little grasp of what was involved, they often agreed to spend this money.

Sometimes, it was a good investment but sometimes not. However, IT departments tended to make their arguments based on the technology itself, without specifically relating it to business strategy, reinforcing the idea that IT was divorced from the business.

As this was happening, the business itself was coming up with more and more requirements for which IT did not have the capacity to develop solutions. Irrespective of whose fault this was it resulted in long backlogs and increased perceived issues with IT.

Then in 1982, Personal Computers (PCs) suddenly became widely available. The business areas outside of IT rapidly adopted them, and the PC revolution began. Software packages could be purchased for PCs that performed all kinds of useful tasks, and IT was no longer needed to develop computerized solutions. The resentment of IT came to the fore, and many IT organizations were split up and farmed out amongst business departments.

The Return of IT

It quickly became apparent that standalone PCs could not provide the functionality required by business departments. The PCs had to "talk to each other," since many different people were involved in the processes they were running. Also, the PC revolution replaced many office workers, such as typists and middle managers, which increased the communication needs of the remaining staff.

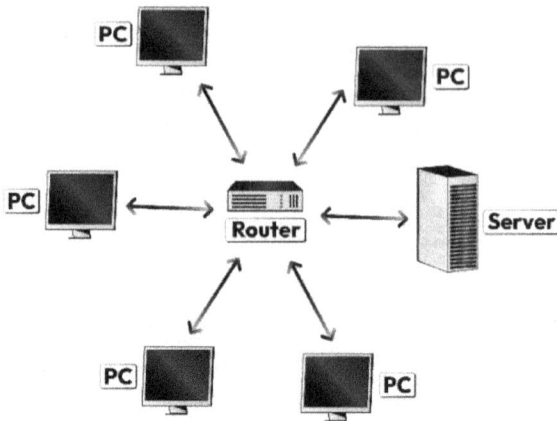

Figure 3.3: Simplified Illustration of a LAN

Technology quickly provided solutions in the form of Local Area Networks (LANs) and client-server architecture, enabling many different PCs to use the same database. Figure 3.3 provides a simplified illustration of a LAN.

This required many technical specialists to implement and maintain the infrastructure. It made no sense to replicate this on a department-by-department basis. It meant having too many technical staff and the risk of different departments using different technologies, which raised overall costs. So centralized IT departments were reconstituted or strengthened, and the business departments got out of the job of running their own computerized resources. By the end of the 1980s, IT was back.

The Rise of Data

While all this was happening, a new idea emerged.

> *The data captured in operational systems might actually have some value beyond enabling the enterprise to complete the transactions in these operational systems.*

For instance, you might track reports of the sales in a particular branch of a big box store and notice that the store rapidly sells out of golf balls every year during the third week of May. Knowing this, you could recommend the business send a much higher supply of golf balls to the store at this time, place the golf balls at the front of the store, and advertise their availability. These actions should increase the sales of golf balls in the store. The data in the reports, rather than on-the-ground knowledge, could be used to increase revenue—an idea that had never occurred to people before.

In parallel with the use of data to increase revenue, other business drivers, such as increasing efficiency and reducing risk, added to the complexity of reporting that began to be needed in enterprises. Complex regulatory reporting requirements began to grow in some industries. From a technical perspective, all of this required integrating data from different sources and managing historical data for trend reporting. But operational systems were never designed for any of this.

It all came to a head in the 1990s with the rapid rise of data warehouses. Data warehouses were built to integrate data from many operational (source) systems, maintain historical data, and rearrange data to produce reports that would satisfy the new reporting requirements. Figure 3.4. provides a simplified view of the processing steps in a data warehouse. The transition from process-centricity to data-centricity had begun.

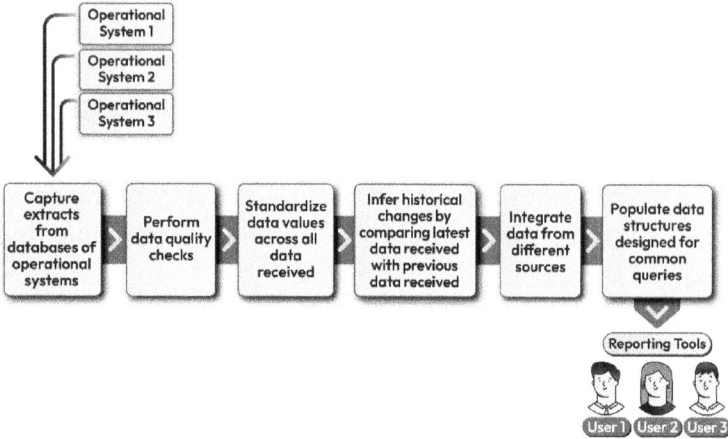

Figure 3.4: Simplified Processing Steps in a Data Warehouse

Data warehouses required even more careful design than the relational databases for operational systems. Without attention to design, data warehouse projects often went spectacularly wrong. The idea that data cannot be reduced to technology became more and more evident. New theories of data modeling specifically for data warehouses were also developed at this time.

The Appearance of Data Administration

Such was the focus on data that a new kind of IT unit dealing solely with data quickly became popular during the 1990s. These were the Data Administration units. Their focus was primarily on:

- Data modeling for the design of new databases, especially data warehouses.

- Data standards, such as naming conventions for database tables and columns.

- The identification and removal of unused database tables and columns.

- The development and maintenance of "metadata repositories," which were usually data dictionaries explaining the business meaning of database tables and columns. A major use was in understanding the data elements in operational systems so they could be used successfully in data warehouses.

The outputs of Data Administration were intended primarily for other staff in IT departments, who were supposed to use the data models to create databases, conform to data standards, get rid of unused tables and columns, and so on. Sometimes, this worked well, but often Data Administration was ignored. That said, Data Administration units were the first widespread organizational structures exclusively dedicated to data.

The Internet, Second Fall of IT, and Extinction of Data Administration

Data warehouses were not the only thing happening in the 1990s. The Internet began, quietly at first, but gaining in momentum to the extent that a massive speculative bubble was inflated by the end of the decade. In those heady days, it seemed that a new Internet startup would replace every traditional enterprise, and massive funds flowed to those startups and the IT departments that were always keen to acquire the latest technology.

But in March 2000, the "dot.com" bubble burst and the reviled "bricks and mortar" traditional business units returned to exact a massive revenge on IT departments. IT budgets were cut everywhere, including those who worked on data-centric projects. This got even worse after the terrorist attacks of September 11, 2001.

Data Administration units were disbanded almost everywhere as part of the cost-cutting exercises needed to compensate for the profligacy of the dot.com bubble. This proceeded in stages to see if there were any negative consequences after the first round of cuts. There were none, so the cuts continued until Data Administration units became extinct everywhere. It was so traumatic that ever afterward, practically nobody spoke of Data Administration or even uttered its name.

The Dark Age and Emergence of Data-Centric Specializations

From 2000 to 2005, nobody seemed to care much about data, but in reality, there was significant progress toward data-centricity as organizations tried to unlock the value of their data.

Master Data Management (MDM) became prominent as new technologies emerged to support it. MDM is the curation of data about things that are important to an enterprise, such as customers and products, rather than data about events, such as sales. It focuses on ensuring that these things are similarly identified in all systems where they are used, and that the data about them can be trusted.

Another data specialization that grew at this time was data quality (DQ). Again, more technologies arose to support it, making it more feasible. DQ seeks to detect incorrect data values and to establish procedures to correct and prevent them from happening again.

The Ascent of Data Governance

By 2005, there was a growing realization that data needed more attention. Organizations had made the commitment to extracting value from data, but had simply acquired technologies to move, store, query, and report on data. Yet many of these initiatives failed to deliver.

> *After spending untold billions of dollars, it became obvious that a lot of data was not understood, and had such enormous DQ issues that it could not be trusted and therefore could not be used.*

As if a tightly coiled spring was suddenly released, Data Governance burst onto the scene. It was a response to the "data mess" in organizations. Very importantly, responsibility for Data Governance was often placed in the business units of organizations, not in IT. This was not true everywhere, and in some places, Data Governance was part of IT, while in others, people from IT were recruited into

Data Governance units in the business (and carried the IT mindset with them). But it was a significant divorce of data and IT.

The concept of Data Governance was still ill-defined, although it had the objective of solving the "data mess." The principal way this was addressed was to set up Data Governance Councils formed of senior managers from business units who met monthly and directed working groups to address data needs.

Data and the Global Financial Crisis (GFC)

In September 2008, the Global Financial Crisis hit. This crisis did not lead to an extinction event for Data Governance, but instead dramatically elevated its role. Prior to the GFC, government regulators had shown little interest in the topic of data. They were certainly highly interested in regulatory reporting, but not data.

Because regulators or governments did not accurately predict the GFC, they began to look for reasons and identified data as one of them. Regulators began to demand that the reports submitted to them be based on data taken directly from the operational systems of financial institutions, without modification, and this had to be proven. Previously, these reports might just be numbers manually entered into a spreadsheet without any description of provenance. Another issue regulators seized on was the accurate identification of counterparties involved in financial transactions, which, as noted earlier, is a goal of MDM.

The result was an increase in Data Governance activities in financial services organizations. The financial services industry does not produce any physical goods and is heavily dependent on data. Therefore, financial services are leaders in data matters that organizations in other economic sectors emulate. This meant that organizations in other sectors began to follow suit.

The Appearance of The Cloud

Another trend that had been in progress for several years by 2008 was Cloud computing. The need for this computing originated with organizations that had to process huge amounts of data, initially a few commercial enterprises and defense and intelligence agencies. They found a way to cheaply scale hardware environments using what was called "junk" hardware in an architecture with failover and hardware replacement. Non-relational databases were implemented that could process queries shaped to the data with lightning speed.

A new generation of technology thus became available, but in addition, huge data centers were built whose computing power could be rented out. Suddenly, businesses did not have to own an "on-premise" data center with all its costs. Instead, they could communicate via the Internet with the resources they needed. Thus, during the 2010s, there began a muti-year migration of systems and data to the Cloud— the new data centers accessed via the Internet.

The non-relational databases turned out to be useful for ingesting datasets. A dataset could simply be stored as a file but viewed as a database table if needed. These environments were dubbed "Data Lakes" and came to rival Data Warehouses. Data Warehouses always had to be built in a forward engineering manner with precise data modeling. Data Lakes, by contrast, had a "storage model" and not a "semantic model," meaning datasets could just be put there and understood later.

This suited IT perfectly. They could adopt the new technology without any need to understand data meaning or requirements. And data lakes were built in many organizations from 2010 onwards.

Data-Centricity Arrives

The data lakes helped enterprises to easily ingest datasets from outside sources, including from many data vendors. A new data discipline of Data Acquisition was developed to manage these processes. In the past, there had always been a few major data vendors that provided specialized data, like Bloomberg, which provided stock prices at market close. But now, a huge number of vendors of "alternative data" (meaning non-traditional data) arose. Some of these were linked to "free" apps downloaded onto smartphones, which tracked the activities of their users. For instance, a fishing gear retailer could, in theory, buy a dataset about when surf fishers visited locations close to their stores, and adapt their marketing campaign accordingly. Data started to become much more of a business than previously, as alternative data was needed for specific analytics.

Public concerns about data surfaced in the European Union after revelations that personal data from social media sites was being sent to US intelligence agencies. These concerns led to establishing the first strong data protection law – the General Data Protection Regulation (GDPR), which came into force in 2018. Any business operating in the European Union had to comply with the regulation. Data Governance units were given the task of implementing compliance.

| 4.5.2016 | EN | Official Journal of the European Union | L 119/1 |

I

(Legislative acts)

REGULATIONS

REGULATION (EU) 2016/679 OF THE EUROPEAN PARLIAMENT AND OF THE COUNCIL

of 27 April 2016

on the protection of natural persons with regard to the processing of personal data and on the free movement of such data, and repealing Directive 95/46/EC (General Data Protection Regulation)

https://eur-lex.europa.eu/legal-content/EN/TXT/PDF/?uri=CELEX:32016R0679

Figure 3.5: Opening Section of the GDPR

The data lakes gradually gave rise to yet another wave of technology dubbed the "modern data stack." These products supported the rapid development of data pipelines – processes to integrate and transform source data for reporting, analytics, and AI.

During the mid-2010s, there were major developments in data science. This involved building predictive models that used the outputs of data pipelines to do things like suggest purchases to customers. At first, highly qualified statisticians were needed to build these models, but Machine Learning (ML) quickly arrived and mostly displaced the data scientists. ML is technology that looks for patterns in data. It can be used to discover correlations between many data elements like customer demographics, and a specific data element like customer spend. No causal analysis is involved, but the correlations can provide pretty accurate predictions, at least for a while. The usefulness of ML led to a huge increase in data pipeline development.

In summary, the decade of the 2010s saw a massive increase in data centricity in organizations. The process centricity that had characterized the start of the computer revolution was greatly diminished.

Data Governance 2.0

By 2010, it became apparent that the initial model of Data Governance based on a Data Governance Council did not work. The members of the Data Governance Council were not data specialists and did not know how to solve data problems.

As a result, specialized Data Governance units started to be implemented, mostly in the business, as IT was felt to be more concerned about technology. These units focused on risk mitigation, especially when it was realized that data privacy laws were coming. However, they also tried to do other things, such as promote data reuse and sharing.

Beginning in 2009, technology support for Data Governance began to appear in the form of what are now called data catalogs. These, to some extent, emulated the old metadata repositories of the era of Data Administration. However, they had much greater functionality and aimed to be used enterprise-wide, even if initially focused on Data Governance units.

Having technology available was a further boost to Data Governance units and helped to make them more relevant. Since the data catalogs aimed to be enterprise-wide, another generation of Data Governance was envisaged to promote data democratization. That is, the information stored in the data catalogs could help business users develop their own data pipelines and help solve their specific needs. This is Data Governance 3.0, and the move to it is still ongoing.

Covid and Artificial Intelligence

The 2020s began with the Covid pandemic. Because of the lockdowns, companies had to ensure their important operations could function via the Internet. A huge wave of digital transformation was sparked as operations were digitized so that staff could work from home and customers could buy goods and services online. Interestingly, many of these efforts were led from within the business as IT was thought to be too slow to produce the required results in time.

New data concerns emerged, such as what data could be stored on a local PC if someone was working at home, and what protective measures should be taken to safeguard data.

After Covid subsided, another new technology suddenly became available for general use in late 2022: Artificial

Intelligence (AI). Again, a huge bubble was inflated as organizations everywhere started to understand AI and determine how they should adopt it. AI mostly requires unstructured data, such as pure text, images, audio, and video. This is not at all like the traditional structured data that sits inside databases. So now there was a need to manage unstructured data in addition to structured data. At the time of writing, the regulatory frameworks are still being developed for AI, but a lot of it deals with understanding the data that goes into AI and building safeguards for this data.

Digital transformation and the general adoption of AI were unexpected developments in the early 2020s, the ramifications of which are still being worked out.

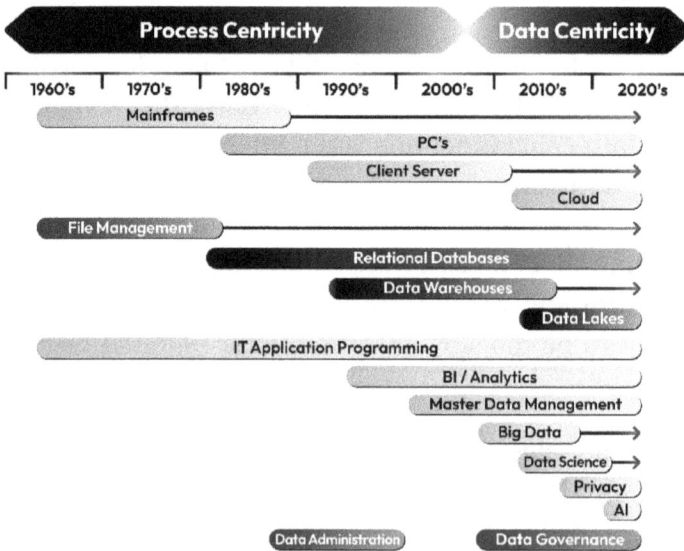

Figure 3.6: Summary Timeline of The History of IT and Data

What Does It All Mean?

This has been a brief and high-level review of the history of data, necessarily omitting various important twists and turns, but what does it all mean? Let's try to synthesize it:

1. Data has gone from being irrelevant to becoming the most important economic resource in the world today. This is because data is used massively for analytics and AI, rather than just transaction processing.

2. About once a decade, there is an event that causes large-scale changes in the role of IT, and these events also impact the organizational units dealing with data.

3. Some data management needs are due to the nature of the technology storing or processing the data, but other needs are completely independent of technology, such as data privacy laws.

4. The complexity of data management needs has risen over time and can be expected to keep rising.

5. As one generation of technology supersedes the previous generations, there is a tendency to forget the learnings from the earlier period. There is no guarantee that this knowledge can be reconstituted at the same maturity level as before.

6. The data mess in most organizations persists and has never been adequately addressed. It grows with technological innovation.

7. Data, at least in terms of its content and meaning, matters more to the business than to IT.

We have described the course of events that has led us to where we are today. It is against this state of affairs that we need to develop and deploy successful data policies.

One of the most powerful reasons for having data policies is the persistence of complexity and issues with data, starting with the introduction of relational databases. Over time, data keeps getting used in new and very important ways, increasing the need for governance and management. Data policies are vital tools to meet these ever-growing requirements.

## Chapter 4

Why Do We Need Data Policies?

This question can be further broken down into:

- Why do we need any policies for data?
- Why do data policies need to be centrally managed by a single unit, such as Data Governance?

Why Do We Need Any Policies for Data?

We have seen that there is general agreement that data is the most valuable resource in the modern economy. But data is not a homogenous substance, like, say, iron. We cannot visualize data, since it has no physical form.

> *We can conceptualize data by defining it and understanding its attributes and relations, but this requires a lot more effort than just picturing something in our minds.*

This effort can help us understand that data cannot manage itself. It can get corrupted, duplicated, or permanently lost. It has to be understood to be used. If it has quality problems, these can have multiplicative effects as the same data can be used infinitely without the data being consumed. There are costs to storing and processing data that need to be managed, and some data can simply be risky to keep around.

These are just a few of the management needs of data, and there are many more. They point to the requirement for a framework to manage data because there are so many needs, and some of them are related. This framework has to be effective within an enterprise setting, meaning that anyone in the enterprise can use it to manage data in acceptable ways. It must be a common framework that applies to everyone in the enterprise. Yes, there can be special needs in particular areas, but we cannot have different organizational units all managing data in divergent ways. That would create chaos.

For data management to be effective, uniform, and understandable by anyone, we need a high-level framework. The solution is to develop a portfolio of data policies. Policies are high-level and, therefore, widely consumable. They can drive consistent data management across the enterprise. There is indeed effort to develop and work with policies. Still, they are a much better alternative than, say, masses of detailed rules that try to be applicable in every specific circumstance but which will never be able to anticipate every situation.

Why Do Data Policies Need to be Centralized?

That answers the first question we posed. But why do data policies need to be centrally managed? Here are some reasons:

1. **Specialization.** If we accept that data is an area of specialization with its own concepts, questions, solutions, patterns, and so on, then we have to arrive at the conclusion that data specialists are needed to deal with it. Data Governance units are formed of these specialists, and are centralized.

2. **Importance.** Few things are more important than data policies because they have such a broad impact since practically everyone in the enterprise works with data. Therefore, it makes sense to have the best specialists develop them. Again, these specialists are located in Data Governance units.

3. **Portfolio.** Data policies also need to be centralized because there is usually a portfolio of these policies that needs to be developed. The scope and content of this portfolio need to be managed, and the development of the policies within it prioritized. The policies have to align without overlaps, gaps, or contradictions. Centralization provides a solution.

4. **User Experience.** There is also the look and feel of policies. These should be consistent from policy to policy. Staff will be irritated if they find one data policy to be in a completely different format from another. Uniformity is most easily achieved via centralization.

Despite these reasons, full centralization may be impossible for some organizations, such as:

- Conglomerates that have very different or highly independent operating companies.

- Huge organizations with very large departments, such as central governments.

- Organizations that operate in different countries, and so have different laws to deal with.

In these situations, it may be possible for some policies to be developed at the parent level, but it will be necessary to develop others at the local level, with the following centralized practices:

1. A centralized Data Governance unit or equivalent must be established at each local level and coordinate effectively with an overall central Data Governance unit at the parent level.

2. The parent level will specify all the standards for the entire policy lifecycle and ensure each local level has the capacity to do policy work following these standards.

3. If it is possible for the parent level to develop a policy then this should always be done, rather than pushing responsibility to the local level.

4. Some policies could be developed at the parent level and subsequently modified at the local level.

5. The parent level will perform quality control on all policies developed or modified at the local level.

This is best achieved by forming the parent Data Governance unit first and then having it instantiate Data Governance units in all local organizations. The exact procedure to do that is beyond this book.

Data Governance Leadership

If we agree that Data Governance is the centralized unit that will issue data policies, then Data Governance must want to do so and have the capacity to do so. Data Governance must assume a leadership role. It cannot wait to be told what to do with data policies, as there is no other unit in a position to do so.

Data policies are not an activity like an IT project where there is a need to "gather requirements" in sufficient detail from knowledgeable users to be able to build something. Instead, Data Governance needs to have the vision and leadership qualities to determine what the portfolio of data policies should be and drive their adoption across the enterprise. This is similar to what other units like Human Resources and Finance do for their specific policies.

Data Governance is supposed to be the unit with expertise about data. It should never need to be told what policies to develop – it should just do the work. Nor should Data Governance put anyone else in the enterprise in the position of instructing them about what policies they may or may not issue. Of course, general approval processes may exist for all policies, but that is a different matter, as we will see in the chapter on policy approval. There may also be exceptions, such as the Legal department informing Data Governance of a new Data Privacy law that requires a policy response. However, these exceptions are isolated and do not apply to data management as a whole.

It is imperative that Data Governance take a leadership role in general, and for data policies in particular. Failure to do so will introduce an organizational gap that will eventually get noticed. The importance of data is well understood now, and executives will easily pick up on the absence of effective data policies. In such a situation, executives will conclude that Data Governance is failing in its mission and may replace the leadership or entire staff.

Taking a leadership stance does not mean that Data Governance should use brute force to implement data policies either. Reasonable, persuasive, and diplomatic approaches should be used, which we will consider in subsequent chapters.

Policies are needed to safeguard the data resources of the entire enterprise, and Data Governance must control them. Centralization requires leadership.

## Chapter 5

The Policy Lifecycle

We have made the case as strongly as we can that data policies are needed. As Data Governance units realize this, there can be a strong temptation to just jump in and start writing policies. As they are written, management can be told about the number that has been created, and perhaps this will make Data Governance look good in management's eyes. But the reality is that a policy document produced as just an artifact, nothing more than a file stored in a directory somewhere, does not affect anybody's behavior. Furthermore, it is not simply a matter of "writing" a policy. A policy has to be developed, operationalized, enforced, and continuously managed. The act of writing is obviously part of that, but in the long run, it is a very small part.

In the Introduction, we discussed the need to institutionalize data policies and make them sustainable, unlike point in time exercises that rarely survive for 18 months and make no significant impact on the enterprise. Institutionalization and sustainability imply robust processes and an architecture for the governance and management of data policies.

> The best architecture and organizing principle for governance and management of data policies is to build on a well-defined policy lifecycle.

A policy lifecycle will consist of a number of phases that must be scrupulously followed to achieve success. The decomposition into phases also allows easier planning for policy work as what is needed is clearer, and the right resources can be mobilized at the right times to do this work. A better policy product is the outcome.

The very worst thing that can happen is to ignore this and just write data policies in an *ad hoc* manner. The chances are that such work products will be poor and the policies will go nowhere. This will diminish the credibility of the Data Governance unit writing the data policies and do nothing to help the enterprise manage data better. It is vital to follow the phases of the policy lifecycle to avoid this outcome.

Figure 5.1 summarizes the policy lifecycle, which consists of 11 distinct phases. In subsequent chapters, we will deal with each phase in detail, but we will briefly summarize them here:

- **Policy Request:** Policy work starts with a formal request of some kind. Very often this is a decision within the Data Governance unit, or equivalent, that is responsible for data policies, but sometimes requests can come from outside this unit. Requests do not have to be for a new policy. They might be to change or discontinue a policy.

- **Policy Formulation:** The development of a new or updated policy, with controls and checks in the drafting process.

- **Policy Harmonization:** The checking that a new or changed policy does not conflict with any other policy. All enterprise policies should be checked, not just data policies. Any conflicts must be resolved.

- **Policy Approval:** The new or updated draft policy goes to any organizational body that is required to approve policies. There may be multiple such bodies. They also have to approve policy discontinuations.

- **Policy Promulgation:** Informing the enterprise about the new, changed, or discontinued policy. This is primarily a communications effort, but sometimes training may be needed for a policy. Support for the policy is also planned for at this point.

- **Policy Operationalization:** It is up to individuals, business units, and teams impacted by the policy to put it into practice. Sometimes, what has to be done is obvious, but sometimes, it is not. Operationalization may vary from context to context.

- **Policy Variance:** If an individual or business unit cannot operationalize part or all of a policy, they can request to be exempted from it for a specific period of time.

- **Policy Compliance Checking:** Someone has to be responsible for checking that the policy is complied with, and they must perform the checks. There can be all kinds of ways of doing this, and automation may be possible for certain data policies.

- **Policy Compliance Follow-up:** This occurs if there is a compliance "finding," that is, an out-of-compliance situation for a particular policy. It is expected that the Data Governance unit will help the business unit that is out of compliance to take action to get into compliance. This is because the Data Governance unit is best placed to explain the policy in detail.

- **Policy Review:** All policies need to be periodically reviewed to ensure they are up to date with business, regulatory, technology, and other realities. If it is felt that a policy needs to be updated or discontinued, a policy request is raised, and the lifecycle begins all over again. In addition to policies, the procedures and organizational structures for governing and managing data policies are also reviewed.

- **Policy Discontinuation:** If a policy is no longer relevant or simply does not work, it must be discontinued. The policy may be replaced by another policy.

Overview of the Policy Lifecycle

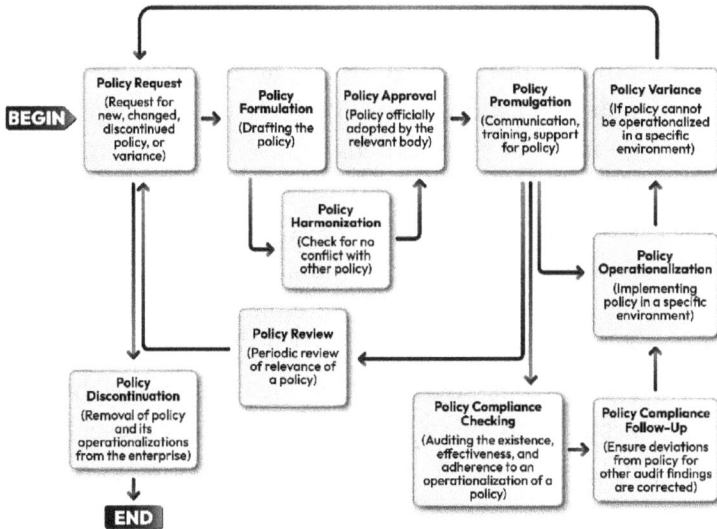

Figure 5.1: The Policy Lifecycle

Preparation for the Policy Lifecycle

Before the Data Governance unit designs a lifecycle for data policies, it must know what external dependencies exist. These external dependencies will require working with other groups who operate independently of Data Governance. Most probably, there will be dependencies with:

- **Policy Harmonization:** Sometimes this is done by a specialized unit, but often not. If it is done by a specialized unit, then Data Governance needs to know how to engage with them. Data Governance also needs to know how far in advance the harmonization group needs to be notified of a new or changed policy, and how long they usually take to perform their tasks.

- **Policy Approval:** Often one or more bodies outside of the Data Governance unit have to approve all policy actions (new, changed, or discontinued). These bodies are usually committees or some kind of working group. Sometimes, it is an individual executive. It is important to know the schedule of meetings and how to get on the agenda. If this is not understood, there is a risk that the meeting cadences of these groups may be so intermittent that unforeseen delays can occur.

- **Policy Promulgation:** Is there a centralized communications group that either has to send out information about a new, updated, or discontinued policy, or which has to be part of the process to do this? Again, the workload and speed of operation of such a group may impact timelines for data policies.

- **Policy Compliance Checking:** Very often, a group like Internal Audit has to check for policy compliance. There may be a formal handoff of a new or updated policy to Internal Audit, and this process may need to be scheduled. Again, timelines may be impacted.

Depending on the enterprise, there may be other specialized units or bodies that have to get involved during these or other phases. All of this must be researched at the outset of policy work by the Data Governance unit. Once the situation is clarified, more detailed design work for a data policy lifecycle can be undertaken, and realistic timeframes can be estimated for policy work.

RACI for Policy Lifecycle

Policy work, at least in terms of formulating new policies or updating existing ones, is rather intermittent. As such, it is worth having something like a checklist to remind everyone of the detailed steps involved, and which individuals, units, and groups need to be part of the process at each step.

The simplest way to capture this information is in a RACI matrix. A RACI matrix is a set of tasks and the people or units involved in the tasks.

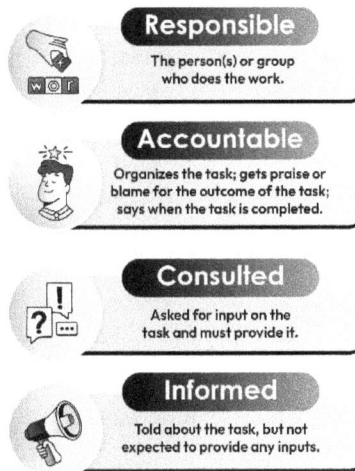

Responsible
The person(s) or group who does the work.

Accountable
Organizes the task; gets praise or blame for the outcome of the task; says when the task is completed.

Consulted
Asked for input on the task and must provide it.

Informed
Told about the task, but not expected to provide any inputs.

Figure 5.2: Summary of Meaning of RACI

Figure 5.2 summarizes the meaning of the acronym "RACI." For each task, there are four types of roles: Accountable, Responsible, Consulted, and Informed.

> *Data Governance should construct the RACI for the entire policy lifecycle.*

This will show who gets involved at each step. The RACI also acts as a checklist so nothing gets forgotten, and it clarifies who does what for each task.

While Data Governance develops the RACI, that does not mean that Data Governance is accountable for each task. As we have noted above, there may be an organizational body outside of Data Governance that has to approve all policies. This body will be both accountable and responsible for the approval task, but Data Governance is not.

A lot more could be written about RACI matrices, but Table 5.1 highlights some of the more important points.

Point	Description
1	There must only be one Accountable (A) per task. If you find the need to have more than one, it probably means the task is not atomic enough. If this occurs, carefully consider the task to determine if it can be broken down into more atomic tasks.
2	An Accountable (A) can also be Responsible (R), but this is the only instance when roles are mixed. Apart from this, the roles of R, A, C, and I are atomic per task. That is, no one person or organizational unit can be assigned more than one role type per task. Of course, many different people or organizational units can be assigned as e.g. "C" for a given task.

Point	Description
3	A RACI is not a flowchart. It helps to have all the tasks in sequential order, but this is a limitation of a RACI. Furthermore, decision points are not really incorporated into a RACI. If you need flow with decision points, then do a flowchart in addition to the RACI. Alternatively, you may find a way to enhance your RACI to show flow, decisions, and branching. However, like everything, the basic RACI concept has limitations.
4	Sometimes, it is obvious which people or organizational units fill the roles for each task. Sometimes, this is not clear, and in these cases, the RACI developer (Data Governance) should assign the Accountable and meet with them to fill out the R, C, and I roles for the task.

Table 5.1: Important Considerations for RACI Matrices

Changing circumstances may affect the policy lifecycle. For instance, as enterprises grow, they can become more serious about policies and establish enterprise-level controls that did not previously exist. Such changes can impact the policy lifecycle. Therefore, Data Governance should undertake an annual review of the policy lifecycle RACI to make sure it is still aligned with the reality of the enterprise and is effectively performing the tasks it is supposed to. Changes can be made at this point. If there is a particularly urgent need, then the RACI can be changed during the year before the annual review. The change process must include the right stakeholders, which might be many of the Accountables in the RACI.

Example of a Policy Lifecycle RACI Matrix

What might a RACI matrix for the policy lifecycle look like? Below is an example fragment for the part of the Policy Request phase. In reality, it might be quite different for any given enterprise, but the example below should help in understanding what is needed.

#	Task	R	A	C	I
1	Policy request				
1.1	Make a request for a policy action (e.g. a new policy)	Requester	Requester (Anyone)		Data Governance Central Administrator
1.2	Log Request	Data Governance Central Administrator	Data Governance Central Administrator		
1.3	Review request for clarity and completeness	Data Governance Central Administrator	Data Governance Central Administrator		
1.4	If needed, ask for further details about request	Data Governance Central Administrator	Data Governance Central Administrator		Requester
1.5	If asked, provide all needed clarifying details	Requester	Requester		Data Governance Central Administrator
1.6	Reject request if it not about policy	Data Governance Central Administrator	Data Governance Central Administrator	Data Governance Lead	Requester
1.7	Add a request to agenda for upcoming meeting of Data Policy Oversight Committee	Data Governance Central Administrator	Data Governance Central Administrator	Secretary of Data Policy Oversight Committee	Requester; members of Data Policy Oversight Committee

Figure 5.3: Example of a RACI Matrix for a Fragment of the Policy Lifecycle

Checking The Validity of the Data Policy Lifecycle

Once the RACI matrix has been developed, Data Governance will have an artifact that clearly shows how it will deal with data policies throughout the policy lifecycle.

However, enterprises are big and complex places, and it is possible that there are constraints on policy work that the

Data Governance unit is not aware of. This would mean that the RACI matrix does not reflect reality. It is, therefore, important to get the RACI matrix validated in order to discover any constraints.

Now, it might seem reasonable to try to find out about such constraints before even developing the policy lifecycle RACI. However, it is a better approach to develop a draft RACI matrix first for the policy lifecycle. A good analyst does not go to someone and ask them for details of how to do something. It is much more effective to present someone with well thought-out details and ask what is wrong.

Who should Data Governance consult with? Candidates are:

- Every organizational body identified in the RACI matrix that is external to Data Governance. It is very important to confirm that the details of these roles have been correctly captured.

- The Risk Department, more specifically Operational Risk. This is because policies are part of what is termed the "Second Line of Defense" in Risk Management. Data has a rather special place in Risk Management, as it is both a source of operational risk and vital in managing risk. The Risk Department thus has a lot of interest in data policies. Data Governance should engage Risk with a well-thought-out approach using the RACI matrix rather than nothing at all. We would expect Risk to review the RACI and point out anything wrong or missing.

- Internal Audit / Compliance Department. They are likely already included in the RACI, but if not, they should be consulted as they may have specifics about how they get notified about policies, or how policies are handed over to them.

- Legal Department. In some organizations such as certain banks, policies and committee structures are subject to governmental regulation. Legal should evaluate the RACI matrix to determine if there are any legal or regulatory implications that Data Governance is unaware of.

As part of this process, Data Governance may find that there are additional organizational units that should be consulted.

Any feedback should be processed and factored back into the RACI if necessary. Data Governance is consulting with these organizations, not looking for approval of the RACI. However, anything they point out that reveals a material deficiency that must be dealt with.

Also, when Data Governance interacts with organizational units that are external to it, some kind of marketing is always involved. This is particularly true if Data Governance has not interacted with a particular unit before, or interacted rarely with it. In these circumstances, an explanation of what Data Governance is and what data policies are should be part of the meeting.

Who Designs the Data Lifecycle?

The lifecycle for data policies is foundational for all data policy governance, so it is essentially a bootstrapping process before the mature procedures can be set up. Clearly, the Data Governance unit is responsible for developing it, and this work should be done as a project as it is time-bounded and there are clear outputs: the lifecycle and RACI matrix.

The work needs to be undertaken by fairly senior members of the Data Governance team who have enough political acumen to be able to recognize and navigate political and bureaucratic issues that might exist in the enterprise. Some junior staff can assist with logistics, notetaking, etc. The effort should not take more than two months elapsed, and hopefully can be completed in a month. It is not a project that requires anyone to work full time on it, but probably eight hours a week is the absolute minimum needed by the participants. Of course, this will vary with each enterprise. The result is that there is a clear high-level picture of all the steps involved in governing and managing data policies, and who is responsible for what.

## Chapter 6

The Policy of Policies

O nce the rough outline of the data policy lifecycle has been developed, it is possible to write the first policy. This first policy is a special one.

> *The first policy must be the "policy of policies" for data.*

This may sound like a very strange concept when it is first encountered, but it is logical and important. Not only is it a policy, but it brings into being the organizational structure and procedures for governing and managing data policies.

The policy of policies includes the following important components:

- The scope of the entire portfolio of data policies. That is, what these policies will cover. It may also be necessary to say what they do not cover.

- The identity of the organizational unit that is primarily accountable for the development and management of the data policies.

- The authority conferred on this organizational unit with respect to the data policies it develops and manages.

- The high-level processes within the policy lifecycle that will be used for developing and managing the data policies, including all roles and responsibilities.

- Additional organizational bodies with specific responsibilities in governing and managing data policies.

Who Writes the Policy of Policies?

The development of the policy of policies is another bootstrapping activity. The policy of policies has to formalize the framework for data policies, but it is itself a data policy, and has to be approved, but the approval mechanism is not yet enshrined in any policy.

There is a further complication. In highly regulated industries, like banking, there is often a prohibition about organizational units granting themselves rights and authority. It is frequently expressed using the metaphor of "the fox guarding the henhouse," although this may not be the best analogy.

The core of the worry is that an organizational unit like Data Governance may set itself up with a policy framework enshrined in a policy of policies that does bad things, like remove checks and balances, or exempt Data Governance from reasonable behaviors that apply to everyone else, or get out of doing work that it really should do.

This is one reason why, in some enterprises, the policy of policies has to be written by a group other than Data Governance. Sometimes, it is an area like the Risk Department. Sometimes, it is a working group that excludes Data Governance and may include external consultants.

This does not mean that Data Governance cannot provide inputs to the policy of policies. It can and should. However, the unit or group writing the policy of policies is free to accept, modify, or reject these inputs. Obviously, Data Governance should ensure that anyone writing the policy of policies for data is fully briefed on the relevant details of data management. Unfortunately, the expertise about data management is usually located in Data Governance. The people writing the policy of policies may be well versed in policy work, but lack data expertise. This is why it is important to brief them. Again, engaging outside consultants with data expertise in this process can be helpful.

Another issue is that if Data Governance is not going to write the policy of policies, it still has to take action to get it written. This will likely require going to the executive level and requesting a project be initiated to write the policy of policies. If it was discovered during the research for the policy lifecycle that there is some overall body that approves all policy-related projects, then this body might be the right one to approach.

In most enterprises, however, Data Governance will be allowed or instructed to write the data policy of policies.

Regulation and Corporate Governance

Yet another complication is the encroachment of government regulation into the data space. This is being fueled in part by governmental responses to a variety of issues, like data privacy and AI. Government regulation also tends to impact corporate governance, which is the overall set of policies, organizational bodies, and practices by which the enterprise is directed and controlled. Thus, government regulation can cause corporate governance to collide with data policies. For instance, there is a regulation in the state of Colorado concerning certain kinds of data that could be used in AI systems. Part of this regulation requires oversight by the Board or a Board committee (see Figure 6.1 below).

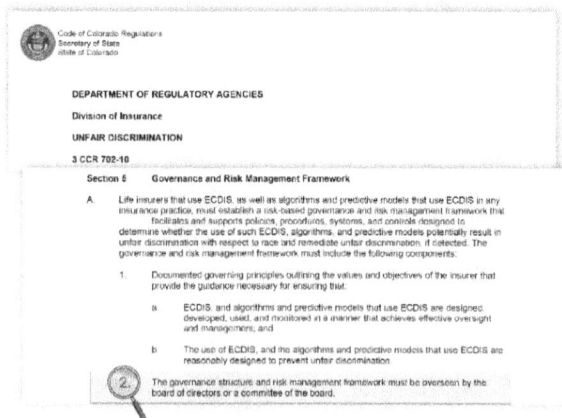

Figure 6.1: Fragment of Colorado Regulation Requiring Board Oversight

It would seem that, in this case, the Board (or Board committee) would have to get involved in the approval of a data policy of policies.

This means that there is a trend of some aspects of Data Governance being increasingly absorbed by more general corporate governance and Data Governance is no longer left to do as it sees fit in the area of data policies. Rather, there will be some degree of participation by corporate governance bodies. It seems reasonable to expect that in the future, overarching matters like a data policy of policies will require approval and may even be written by corporate governance bodies. For now, however, that seems not to be the norm and writing the data policy of policies is the responsibility of Data Governance.

The Scope of Data Policies

The policy of policies must clearly specify the domain of the enterprise activities that data policies apply to. This should be the same as the domain within which data governance and data management tasks occur, and should be the same as prescribed in any remit for the Data Governance unit.

Two immediate problems to be avoided are:

- Setting the scope of data policies too broadly, and thus getting into conflicts with other policy areas that really are distinct from data.

- Setting the scope of data policies too narrowly so there are gaps in how data governance and data management activities should be properly carried out.

However, data is everywhere in the enterprise, so the most probable risk is setting the scope too narrowly. As long as it is clearly stated that the scope is strictly limited to data, the scope should not be overly broad.

> Nevertheless, the problem of other organizational units that issue data policies is a real one, irrespective of the policy scope assigned to in the policy of policies.

After all, Data Governance is a relative newcomer as an organizational unit, and other units will have been forced to deal with data needs at the policy level in the past.

For instance, the Information Security unit in IT has the task of protecting sensitive data. What is sensitive data? Typically, Information Security will develop a policy to classify data into various levels of sensitivity. This is a data governance policy, but clearly not issued by the Data Governance unit.

It may not be that easy to decide what a "data policy" is and what it is not, but the scope of what is to be considered as a data policy must be defined in the policy of policies. One way to do that is as follows:

- All general data governance and data management policies are in scope.

- Specific data governance and data management policies that require specialized capabilities that reside in a unit outside of Data Governance are out of scope. This is like the example of the Data Classification Policy issued by Information Security. However, the Data Governance unit is to be consulted on these policies.

- Specific data governance and data management policies that are truly unique to a particular area of the enterprise and have been assigned to this area by a higher authority are out of scope, but the Data Governance unit is to be consulted on them if they are out of scope. This situation should be rare.

- Policies that do not deal with general data governance and data management tasks, but which contain statements that incidentally refer to data are out of scope. The Data Governance unit may be consulted on them.

Accountable Organizational Unit

Normally, the Data Governance unit is accountable for data policies. After all, it is the unit that has the primary responsibility for ensuring the availability and trustworthiness of the enterprise data resource. It may not always be called "Data Governance" and such names can change over time. Many years ago, these units were called "Data Administration," and in the future, some other name may replace "Data Governance."

That said, in some organizations with a Data Governance unit, data policies may be the responsibility of some other unit, such as Operational Risk. The desire here seems to be the centralization of many policies that are deemed to have a common theme, such as risk mitigation. If this happens, which is not very common, then the other unit will likely have its own policy of policies and way of policy management.

However, what the other unit will not have is expertise in data governance and data management. Therefore, the Data Governance unit will be needed to develop and manage the data policies. This may be why, in some enterprises, Data Governance is taken over by the Risk Department.

We will not further consider the option of a unit other than Data Governance being accountable for data policies.

Conferring of Authority for Data Policies

With the scope of data policies set, and the Data Governance unit (or equivalent) identified as accountable for data policies, the policy of policies must also include the conferring of the authority for data policies to the Data Governance unit. Figure 6.2 illustrates one possible organizational arrangement for conferring this authority by establishing a data policy of policies.

Ideally, the part of the enterprise that is conferring the authority will be identified. This part of the enterprise must, of course, be in a position to confer the authority. As a consequence, the policy of policies has to be approved by at least this part of the enterprise, if not authored by it. Obviously, the executive level will be the usual part of the enterprise to confer the authority, but this may not be the case in every enterprise.

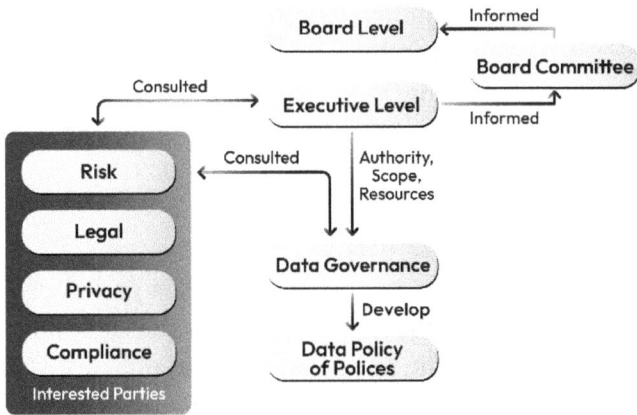

Figure 6.2: Possible High-Level Organizational Arrangements for Developing Data Policy of Policies

It may be optionally stated that the authority is conferred for a fixed period, and is periodically renewable thereafter, subject to review by some organizational body. Alternatively, it may simply be stated that the authority can be removed by the part of the organization conferring it with or without some notice period.

The Policy Lifecycle and Operating Model

A major part of the policy of policies is to provide details of how data policy work will be done.

We have already discussed the policy lifecycle, which is the conceptual framework for policy work. There does not have to be a lot of detail about processes in the policy of policies, but the overall phases of the policy lifecycle, the organizational bodies involved, and the responsibilities of these bodies should be laid out.

The organizational bodies (the operating model) for data policies is described in detail in the next chapter and is a very important part of the policy of policies.

Approval and Review

The organizational body that approves the data policy of policies should be named in the policy of policies. Usually, a statement is also included to say that this body has sole responsibility for any interpretation of the policy of policies.

A statement about the review cycle for the policy of policies should be included since the policy of policies is managed outside of the normal data policy lifecycle.

Policy of Policies vs. Data Governance Charter

While we have been considering the policy of policies as a standalone document, there is one variation that is implemented in some organizations. This is where the content of the policy of policies is put into the charter for a Data Governance unit. The charter is the foundational document that establishes a Data Governance unit. It describes the vision, mission, structure, and reporting relationships of the unit, but can optionally cover data policies too.

The advantage of this approach is that everything in terms of the setup of the Data Governance unit gets done in one document at one time. The disadvantage is that there are a lot of specific considerations for data policies that really do not fit in a charter, but should be in a policy of policies. The policy of policies should be allowed to change independently of the charter that establishes Data Governance. Such changes may be needed more frequently than changes to a charter as data policy processes are optimized over time. Also, as we have pointed out, some organizations require there to be a separate policy of policies.

Therefore, this book recommends a distinct policy of policies for data policies. If an enterprise requires everything to be in the charter for the Data Governance unit, this can still be accommodated, but may not be optimally efficient.

The "Data Governance Policy"

One strange idea that is sometimes encountered is that there should be a single "Data Governance Policy." This seems to be a single all-encompassing policy for everything within the scope of data governance and data management. Such "policies" can be enormously long. Obviously, they are ineffective and very difficult to create and maintain. This book takes the approach that distinct areas of data governance and data management require their own individual policy. We will not consider the single unified "Data Governance Policy" further.

Additional Details

We have not covered everything that needs to go into the policy of policies in this chapter. Subsequent chapters include suggestions for additional content related to specific phases of the policy lifecycle and certain standards needed for data policy work.

Final Approval

After the data policy of policies has been drafted, it should be approved. The audience is mainly the Data Governance unit, so there is usually no need for any large-scale promulgation. However, it is probably wise to inform all the other organizational units and groups mentioned in the policy of policies.

Now that we have seen how to develop the policy of policies, we will look more closely at the organizational structures that it must establish to do data policy work.

## Chapter 7

Organizational Framework for Data Policies

The policy of policies establishes the scope and authority for data policies, but it also has to establish the organizational framework for governing and managing data policies. Sometimes this is called the "institutional framework" or "operating model," and it is a very important part of the policy of policies.

However, it is also often controversial. This book aims to provide a strategy to build an unstoppable machine for the operationalization and management of data policies that will be successful and sustainable because it transcends any individual and is deeply embedded in the enterprise. This requires organizational bodies whose purpose is to drive data policies. Some people react against this, feeling it is bureaucratic and not "pragmatic." Indeed, it is bureaucratic in the sense that a formal operating model is established, but this is necessary for smooth administration in all forms of governance. And it is not "pragmatic" in the sense that it is not *ad hoc*, does not lack checks and balances, and is not dependent on specific individuals.

The Data Policy Oversight Committee

There has to be one body that oversees data policy work.

It is unlikely that the Data Governance unit will go rogue and start creating policies that are impossible to comply with, but Data Governance itself cannot certify it is creating sensible data policies and following all required procedures.

Data Governance should not approve its own work. Data policies are simply too important and have such widespread impact that they require oversight.

A reasonable approach is for the policy of policies to establish a Data Policy Oversight Committee. This committee will deal with all oversight actions and some of the important management actions related to data policies.

Again, it may seem that establishing a formal committee is overly bureaucratic and risks introducing unnecessary overhead and delays. Of course, this is possible if the committee is run very badly, but not because of the actual concept of such a committee, which has the following advantages:

- **Transparency:** It is very clear who is directing the production of data policies. Without something like a committee, it may be unclear what decisions are being taken around data policies, and who is taking them. Such opaqueness can lead to a poor reputation for Data Governance and a lack of receptivity to data policies by the staff in the enterprise.

- **Audit Trail:** The decisions of the committee will be published in the minutes of its meetings, which provides transparency as well as an audit trail of what decisions were taken, when they were taken, and why they were taken. Ideally, the minutes of meetings will be made available generally so all staff can see them, further adding to transparency.

- **Consultation:** The makeup of the committee can be drawn from Data Governance, but it is very beneficial to include staff from other areas, such as Legal, Risk, and so on. This will bring additional perspectives and experience to the committee.

Composition of the Data Policy Oversight Committee

The Data Policy Oversight Committee should include senior staff from Data Governance. Since Data Governance has the expertise about data, it must have this representation.

Ideally, the committee will be chaired by the head of Data Governance. This will ensure that the decisions of the committee will get actioned by Data Governance efficiently. The head of Data Governance will also be in a better position to understand the details of policy work more than anyone else who might be a candidate to chair the committee.

A secretary from Data Governance is also needed to schedule meetings, set meeting agendas, and write and distribute minutes. Depending on the enterprise, the secretary may or may not be able to vote. Other representatives from Data Governance who specialize in the policy area should also be included on the committee.

However, the committee cannot have representation from Data Governance alone. If that were the case, we would be back to Data Governance overseeing itself. Outside representation will help bolster the prestige of the committee, which is important. There will also be a reduced need to consult later on with these other areas of the enterprise, given that they have representation on the committee.

Criteria for representation from outside Data Governance could include the following:

- Any unit that has general responsibilities for policies (not just data policies) should be represented. For instance, the Risk Department will be interested generally in policies.

- Any unit that has a specific interest in data policies should be represented. For instance, the Legal Department will be interested in Data Privacy which will inevitably be addressed via one or more data policies.

- Any unit that has an interest in how policies are governed. That is, apart from any interest in the content of policies, the unit is interested in the quality and robustness of the governance and management of the data policy processes. For instance, Regulatory Affairs may need to document the quality of data policy processes.

- Any unit that will be involved in checking compliance with data policies, like Internal Audit.

The number of members from outside Data Governance should be sufficient to overcome any objection that Data Governance is overseeing its own work.

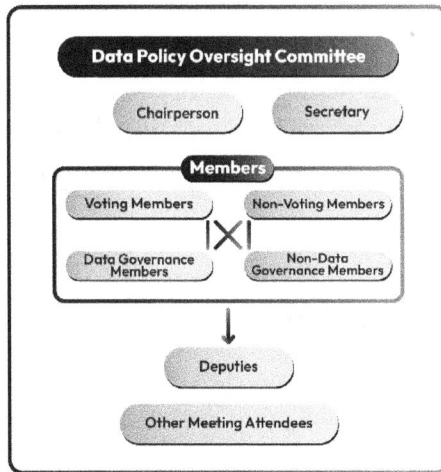

Figure 7.1: Schema of Possible Composition of Data Policy Oversight Committee

Figure 7.1 presents an illustration of a possible composition of the Data Policy Oversight Committee.

For committee members drawn from outside Data Governance, it is important to establish that they represent the areas they work in, and do not serve on the committee in a purely personal capacity. If they were to serve only in a personal capacity, then their respective areas could disavow decisions of the committee.

Additionally, care must be taken with respect to voting rights. Anyone on the committee from outside Data Governance and who has to enforce the data policies should not be permitted to vote. This usually means Internal Audit, Compliance, or similar organizations. The reason is that they could influence policies to make them easier to enforce.

Other subtle corporate governance concerns might impact the structure and operation of the Data Policy Oversight Committee. It is best to consult with Legal before setting up the committee to ensure there are no such issues. Such consultation has to be done as the policy of policies is being formulated because the mandate of the Data Policy Oversight Committee will have to be included in it.

Additional Data Policy Oversight Committee Considerations

Committees may be subject to special scrutiny in some highly regulated industries, such as banking. For instance, regulators may need to be aware of all committees, and the minutes of any committee may need to be distributed to the regulators. There may be some reluctance to create yet another committee in these industries because of the overhead involved. Despite this, the Data Policy Oversight Committee really ought to be a committee because:

- It consists of members from different organizational units, and so it is a very serious endeavor that needs maximum formality.

- The oversight function is very important, as are data policies, and that must be recognized.

- We want to institutionalize data policies to make them sustainable. A committee provides a significant obstacle to *ad hoc* treatment of data policies, and forces procedures to be followed rather than ignored.

The Data Governance Committee/Council

Another suggestion often encountered is that a Data Governance Committee (sometimes called the Data Governance Council) be used to oversee data policies. We discussed Data Governance Committees briefly in the chapter on the history of data. They were originally conceived as directing all data governance work in the enterprise, but later, they were taken over by centralized Data Governance units.

However, one huge advantage of getting the Data Governance Committee to do data policy work is that the need for a Data Governance Committee seems to be almost unquestioned in most enterprises. The likely reason is that the concept of a Data Governance Committee is found in many online and published sources about Data Governance. We will not argue about the general merits and demerits of a Data Governance Committee, but if it is easy to establish to do the work of the Data Policy Oversight Committee, then that is probably the best practical route to follow, and no special Data Policy Oversight Committee is needed.

Having a specialized Data Policy Oversight Committee, irrespective of any Data Governance Committee, is probably the ideal course of action to follow. For the remainder of this book, we will stick with the concept of the Data Policy Oversight Committee. Still, we should keep in mind that in some and perhaps many enterprises, the actual body may be the Data Governance Committee.

Data Policy Oversight Committee Operational Details

The policy of policies will need to include details about how the Data Policy Oversight Committee works, including:

- How long members can serve for.
- Whether members can send deputies in their place, including to vote.
- If there is a fixed schedule of meetings.
- How meeting agendas are set, and how long before a meeting they have to be circulated.
- If there is a quorum for a meeting.
- How voting is carried out.

- If there is an escalation point for matters that cannot be decided.
- Who the minutes are distributed to, and how long after a meeting this is to be done.
- Where agendas and minutes are stored.

There may be many other details, too.

That concludes how we will deal with oversight, but what about the actual policy work? We will deal with that next.

The Data Policy Operations Committee

Data Governance will have to do at least the bulk of the data policy work. Staff in this unit will be assigned tasks, and managers will have to make sure that they are completed on time with the required quality.

In general, data policy work is not a series of projects but is a set of continuously running administrative processes.

From time to time, there may be a project to build something new in terms of organizational structures, procedures, or technology, but in the steady state, this is very much the exception. Nor is it the case that policy work is siloed at the level of the individual. The tasks involved very often require working with other staff members both within Data Governance and outside it.

This means that there has to be an organizational framework for Data Governance to plan and coordinate data policy work, as well as deal with issues that arise. Such administrative work ensures that things run smoothly and in a steady state. It is not a time-bound project, so some other approach is needed.

A reasonable answer is for Data Governance to have an internal Data Policy Operations Committee. However, this committee is significantly different from the Data Policy Oversight Committee. Its characteristics are:

- It exists to facilitate data policy work in Data Governance, and includes only Data Governance staff who work on data policies.

- It helps coordinate the work on data policies within Data Governance so that staff are not working in isolation and provides them with any help they need.

- It develops plans for uniform procedures to do data policy work, implements these procedures, makes sure they are followed, and periodically reviews the procedures to optimize them.

- It is chaired by the head of Data Governance who is the only approval authority. There is no voting.

- There is a secretary who develops agendas, takes minutes, and publishes the minutes.

- The committee meets at least once a month and more frequently if needed.

- It can forward matters to the Data Policy Oversight Committee.

The alternative to a committee is for Data Governance to simply do data policy work as part of its normal function. This would still require meetings and should generate appropriate documentation. However, it would not be transparent, and the decision-making framework would not be clear. It is also likely that the documentation would be inadequate and there would not be an audit trail. Data policies are too important to deal with in this way, and though yet another committee represents some overhead, it is worth it.

The Data Policy Operations Committee does not report to the Data Policy Oversight Committee and does not have to provide inputs to the latter for every meeting. However, it should provide inputs if it determines there is any need to change the overall policy management processes, and it should certainly provide an annual evaluation report for how data policies are being managed. There can be other inputs, too. Figure 7.2 illustrates the relationships between the committees and Data Governance.

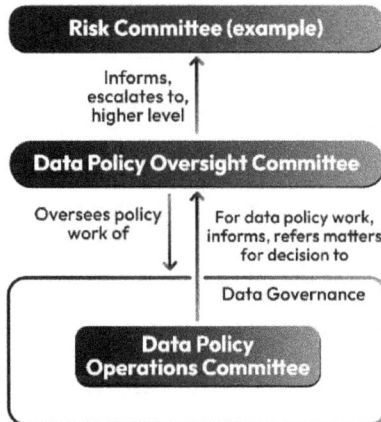

Figure 7.2: Relationships of Data Policy Committees and Data Governance

The Data Policy Oversight Committee has to approve the recommendations of the Data Policy Operations Committee for process improvements, as it oversees the policy management processes.

Like the Data Policy Oversight Committee, the establishment of the Data Policy Operations Committee has to be specified in the policy of policies. We have discussed quite a lot of what the committee does here, but there will be additional elements in subsequent chapters.

## Chapter 8

Principles

What is a Principle?

We define "principle" as:
a statement of fundamental belief that cannot be
further analyzed, and must be accepted as true or
false.

All human actions ultimately rest on principles, even if we do not always realize this is the case. In fact, many principles go unstated, which can be problematic.

One of the main practical values of principles is that they can guide actions where there are no precise rules. Principles also have an important relationship with policies, but to understand this, let's first look at some examples of principles within data management.

The Reality of Principles

Thinking about data, we might formulate the following principle:

Everyone in the enterprise has personal responsibility for the quality of the data they produce.

That sounds fine, but it is only a sentence we have written down. Do not think that principles have to be "good," but never "bad." They can be either—they simply reflect the fundamental bases of our actions.

Returning to the principle we just formulated, we might observe the reality in our enterprise is that frontline workers are told by their managers to push through as many transactions per hour as possible. There may be metrics that track this. So, in practice, transaction volume and timeliness are important, but quality is not. How can this be reconciled with the principle "Everyone in the enterprise has personal responsibility for the quality of the data they produce." In short, it cannot.

The real principle at work in the enterprise is something like:

Produce data to process transactions as quickly as possible.

There is no concern about quality. This real principle would likely never be explicitly stated, as it sounds terrible. However, it still remains as an unstated principle that has a widespread effect on behavior across the enterprise. It is an unstated principle I have actually seen at work in several enterprises.

Therefore, no matter how much we might want principles to be agreeable statements about perfection, they are realities that need to be understood. We talk about "corporate culture," but what we really mean by this, at least in a large part, is the set of principles that are the fundamental basis for how actions are guided across the enterprise. It can be extremely hard to capture the principles that underly corporate culture and write them down because they are unstated and most of the staff are not intellectually aware of them.

The actions of the staff may nevertheless be fully aligned with these unarticulated principles, which can only be inferred by observing how people behave within the enterprise. This is one of the reasons why Organizational Change Management (OCM) is so difficult.

Every Data Governance unit will need to determine what its principles are. Table 8.1 summarizes why this is important.

Principles are important for Data Governance because:

1. They articulate the values espoused by the Data Governance Program.
2. They provide guidance for individuals in situations where there are no specific rules.
3. They are an early way in which the Data Governance Program can be operationalized.
4. They provide a framework in which more detailed directives, especially policies, can be developed.
5. They assist in implementing the vision and mission of Data Governance.
6. They are a way of explaining what Data Governance does.

Table 8.1: Summary of Why Principles are Important for Data Governance

Relationship of Principles to Policies

Now we have reviewed principles in more detail, we are better able to understand their relationship to policies. A data policy states what has to be done with data, not how to do it. But why are we instructing people in the enterprise to manage data in a certain way? There must be a reason for it.

This is where principles come in. The data policies are aligned with our principles about data and likely our corporate principles too.

> *A policy cannot exist in a vacuum but must be there for a reason, and that reason is a fundamental belief we have about data—a principle.*

It may be possible to have a principle for which there are no policies. The principle may only serve as general guidance. However, it is not possible to have a policy that is not aligned to one or more principles, unless the policy is required by something outside the enterprise, like a regulation. Incidentally, some regulations are principles-based rather than rules-based, so even some policies required for regulations align with principles, albeit external ones.

For simplicity, we will only consider policies in the context of the principles explicitly adopted by Data Governance for the remainder of this chapter.

If a particular data policy does not align to any stated data principle, then we have a policy that is based on one or more unarticulated principles, which is something we do not want.

Making sure data policies are always aligned with data principles requires constant vigilance. It is too easy to get sidetracked into formulating a policy for some emergency or tactical need that is not based on the articulated data principles of the enterprise, but on some unarticulated and damaging principle.

This approach of specifying principles and then developing policies has also been used in constructing legal frameworks for thousands of years. It is not something new or unique to data. All the more reason to develop principles and then policies.

Analysis of Principles

As mentioned earlier, principles are statements (propositions) that cannot be further analyzed and just have to be accepted as true or false.

This bothers some people who want to keep asking "Why?." But there is no answer to "why" at some point. While principles cannot be analyzed, their consequences can be understood and evaluated. This is not the same thing as analyzing a principle, but it is very important. As an example, let us go back to the *de facto* principle we discussed before:

Produce data to process transactions as quickly as possible.

This principle says nothing about data quality, but we also know that work that is rushed will contain errors. If we do indeed find data quality errors in the transaction data concerned, we can make a reasonable guess that it is because of the principle. We could interview staff responsible for the transactions to confirm our suspicion.

Therefore, while principles cannot be further analyzed, we can and should measure their effects.

Scope of Data Principles

We are concerned about data principles, and we need to be careful to keep within the scope of data. That is, our principles must be for data and not more general, since Data Governance does not have the authority or expertise to deal with more general concerns. Of course, there is a wider world beyond data, but it is beyond Data Governance's job.

At the same time, the general principles of the enterprise (stated or unstated) may affect data management within the enterprise, and we have to recognize that. In the end, we need adequate data management principles and may need to advocate for them over time, even if there are more general principles at work in the enterprise that are not aligned.

Guiding Principles

Another wrinkle of principles is that there are actually different types. In science, we can find principles that underlie a discipline, such as Newton's Laws of Motion in physics. These are foundational or first principles. In data management, we are concerned with guiding principles. That is, principles that can be used to constrain our actions.

It is not possible to provide detailed rules for how to act in every possible situation in Data Management, or in life for that matter. There are all kinds of specific circumstances where we will need to decide how to act, but no specific guidance is available. This is where guiding principles come in. They can be used to help us judge what the best course of action might be. Figure 8.2 illustrates guiding principles in action.

Figure 8.2: Example of The Effect of a Guiding Principle

Should There be a Data Principles Campaign?

Given the clear usefulness of guiding principles, the question naturally arises as to whether these should be actively promoted by Data Governance or not. We have discussed the use of principles internally by Data Governance to help formulate policies, but if they are so good, why not spread them across the entire enterprise?

If data principles are to be promoted, then we require a strategy for continuous and consistent communication of the data principles. There is really no other way, except perhaps for leading by example, to get the principles embedded in the enterprise.

The issue with such a broad communications effort is that it runs the risk of being disconnected from other communications campaigns, such as data literacy or raising awareness of the Data Governance function. Rather than end up with many disconnected communications campaigns, it is better to plan a single campaign from the start that covers everything that is needed.

There are scaled-back approaches that may be useful, too. Rather than a dedicated campaign, messages about data principles could be folded into communications intended for other purposes. For instance, Data Governance should have an Intranet site, and there could be a page for the principles there. If a communications campaign for Data Literacy is developed, it could include something about the principles on which it is based. Data Quality training could describe the principles that are relevant in this area.

The decision to have a formal communications campaign specifically for principles needs to be weighed against other communications needs that it might crowd out. Perhaps introducing elements about principles into other campaigns is a better solution, but this depends on the enterprise.

Principles Statements

We can summarize how principles statements should be formulated as described in Table 8.2:

Principle Statements should be:

• Extremely clear so they can be easily understood and no technical jargon
• Short, so they are easily remembered and no lists of things
• Action-oriented so they can easily be applied and not theoretical
• Achievable in the current state and oriented to behavior and not dependent on some future Utopia

Table 8.2: Some Best Practices for Developing Principles Statements

An issue with being short is that while it helps memorization, it does not provide an explanation. An explanation will help readers to understand the principle statement better. Table 8.3 has a few examples of data principle statements with explanations.

While brevity is good, we sometimes see single words used for principles, like "quality." This leaves too much to the imagination of the reader and is not a good idea. Principles should be expressed as complete, albeit short, sentences.

1. **Principle: Data Governance is transparent.** This speaks to the way we deal with decisions about data. The enterprise relies on data, and staff should know how decisions were taken about the data they depend on. Of course, there may be limits to transparency because some data is confidential.

2. **Principle: We are accountable for the quality of the data we produce.** As individuals, we are creating new data every day. We must make sure that this is of the highest quality. This will allow everyone to trust in the data that they use.

3. **Principle: We are responsible for the data we use.** When we come to use data, it is important to make sure we really understand what it means, and whether it has been subject to material changes as it has been processed within the enterprise. Not only must we ensure the data is a good fit for the task at hand, but we must also ensure that the way we intend to use the data is legal and ethically responsible.

4. **Data Governance is collaborative.** The same data can be used in many different places, and so when we make plans for data, or need to make decisions about data, it is important to make sure all stakeholders are consulted.

Table 8.3: Principles with Explanations

Formulating Principles

Having described the background of data principles, we now need to focus on how to formulate them. There are two critical success factors that must be in place to do this:

- A deep understanding of data governance and data management.

- A deep appreciation of the business strategy and culture of the enterprise.

A big mistake is to think that the data principles to be formulated are something like happy marketing talk that is intended to create a positive feeling among employees of the enterprise. It is quite possible that some of the principles could be rather tough and may not make average employees happy.

> *Data principles are what we fundamentally believe about data in the context of the enterprise, irrespective of any emotional impact they may have.*

However, a degree of pragmatism needs to be brought to bear on the formulation process. Let us take the example of the principle:

Every individual is responsible for the quality of the data they produce.

This might be difficult to realize in an enterprise that is highly consensus-driven and where responsibility gets diffused via endless meetings to consider decisions. Employees in such an enterprise will not be used to taking accountability. There may be a *de facto* principle at work, such as:

Staff will not willingly take accountability for anything.

Therefore, while we might think our data quality principle is good, we need to determine if it is feasible to use as a basis for policies and standards. Perhaps in some organizations, there is the possibility of effecting the Organizational

Change Management (OCM) to get to the point where staff will take personal responsibility for the quality of data they produce. But in other organizations, it might not be possible in an acceptable timeframe, and might not even be possible at all. Therefore, pragmatic aspects of the ability to get principles adopted across the enterprise must be considered, and this will impact what policies can get successfully operationalized.

With regard to a deep understanding of data governance and management, another issue can be that the Data Governance unit staff are all fairly new to the discipline and lack the required understanding. In such circumstances, outside consultants with this knowledge can be brought in to help formulate the principles. However, the Data Governance staff must know the enterprise strategy and culture to assess whether the principles will work.

From this discussion, we have seen that principles must be developed before data policies. The policy of policies should specify this, and the Data Policy Oversight Committee should approve a set of data principles before any further policy work begins. The Data Governance unit should be mandated to produce the data principles. Since the principles are such an important component of policy work, the Data Policy Oversight Committee should be directed in the policy of policies to get the principles produced, and ensure their curation after they are approved. This will guarantee that the principles are not developed as a point-in-time exercise and forgotten as time passes.

Living by the Data Principles

It is very important that the Data Governance unit actually lives up to the data principles. This is not only an ethical duty, but staff outside Data Governance will pick up on any behaviors by Data Governance that deviate from the principles. The more formal a campaign to spread the principles, the greater the responsibility of Data Governance to be seen living up to them.

Very rarely, the principles that are arrived at may be radical, involve security or confidentiality matters, or be connected to an unannounced business strategy. In these and similar cases, not only may a formal campaign to spread the principles be inappropriate, but any communication about the data principles will need to be controlled. Over time, the principles can be communicated in a careful manner as the enterprise is able to digest them.

Updates to Principles

It is unlikely that once a principle is formulated, it will need to be changed. If it happens, then it will ripple into the policies based on it, which is a good reason to make sure the principles are sound to begin with.

Much more likely is the need for additional principles. Data has seen the growth of important new areas of, such as Data Privacy and Artificial Intelligence (AI). These new areas are either an addition to the overall practices of data governance and data management like Data Privacy, or the emergence of new technology that is in part strongly data-driven like AI. Either way, a policy response is required, and therefore, new principles need to be formulated.

The Data Policy Operations Committee must conduct an annual review of principles that revalidates that the existing principles are appropriate for the enterprise and identifies any reason that new principles are needed or existing ones need to be revised. The results must be reported to the Data Policy Oversight Committee. If the Data Policy Operations Committee becomes aware of any need to change the data principles between reviews, then it must bring this to the attention of the Data Policy Oversight Committee as soon as possible.

## Chapter 9

The Data Policy Portfolio

The data policy of policies provides a description of the scope of data policies, but what does "scope" mean in practice? Ultimately, it is going to be the entire collection or portfolio of data policies.

The Data Governance unit can simply tackle policies one-by-one as it sees needs arising, and grow the portfolio organically. Such a route is taken in many organizations, and in the steady state it makes a lot of sense.

> However, at the beginning of policy work a better approach is to identify all the required policies, prioritize them, and plan for their development.

In this way any dependencies between policies can be understood at the outset, resources needed to develop policies can be mobilized, and data policies that are most urgently needed by the enterprise can be tackled first. Of course, it is impossible to predict all the data policies that will be needed by the enterprise, but such an initial exercise can identify a reasonable set to start working on.

Planning the Policy Portfolio

How are the initial set of policies identified? Obviously, this is an important step, so it needs to be decided carefully.

Firstly, the Data Policy Oversight Committee should make the decision whether or not to identify an initial portfolio of data policies. It is possible that in some enterprises there are overriding circumstances that will only permit data policies to be developed one-by-one, and starting with an initial set is not possible.

We will assume the Data Policy Oversight Committee decides to move ahead with an initial portfolio of data policies. The best option is to give the task to the Data Policy Operations Committee. This is the focus of data policy work in Data Governance, has links to the Data Policy Oversight Committee, and has resources dedicated to policy work. By assigning the task to the Operations Committee, the Oversight Committee forces a collective responsibility on Data Governance, in the sense that the task is not being given to a single individual in Data Governance.

It is very important to bear in mind that this is an initial list of data policies. As such it should be focused on policies for well-known data management tasks. Either the enterprise will already have policies for these tasks, or it will not. Existing policies that cover data management tasks are discussed in the chapter on taking over data policies. This leaves the obvious data management tasks that lack policies. Later on, after all these foundational policies are developed and have been operationalized, Data Governance can start to work on more subtle areas where data management behaviors are inadequate and identify policy gaps. At the outset, however, it is important to concentrate on well-understood and unambiguous policy needs.

Since there is a well-known set of data management tasks that have to be carried out, we would expect the Data Policy Operations Committee to know what many of these are. Of course, due diligence and research should be carried out on what are currently considered to be data management tasks that are relevant to the enterprise. For instance, regulations that require data policies to be developed tend to change quite frequently, so due diligence has to be carried out to determine if there are any unmet policy needs due to regulations.

The Data Policy Operations Committee should also try to find out what senior managers and executives think are priorities for data policies, as they may be seeing things that Data Governance is not. It would be unwise to publish a portfolio of proposed data policies only to have senior managers and executives ask why missing policies were not considered. Note that interactions with higher-level staff always have a marketing component, so a standard explanation should be created of what the exercise to develop a portfolio of data policies is all about. This can be delivered during meetings with senior managers and executives. There may also be an urgent need for specific data policies due to pressing circumstances in the enterprise. Again, these may be driven by regulations that are not yet fully complied with. Or perhaps there is a particular data mess in some area.

The initial list does not have to be complete. There may be some complex data management tasks that require further evaluation to determine if a policy is needed for them. Nor do all of the data principles need to have supporting policies at the outset. We need to aim for a reasonably complete set of proposed policies that address important data needs that we can push through the policy lifecycle in the next 12-18 months, or any objective timeline.

Managing the Policy Portfolio

With the approach described above, the enterprise will be able to develop an initial set of proposed policies that can be formulated. When work will actually start on each of these policies needs to be determined, as resources are always limited. Since we are at the very outset of policy work, the policies that are easiest to develop and least controversial are probably the best choice.

In fact, it is probably an even better idea to pick just one such policy and develop it to the point of operationalization in order to evaluate just how well the processes in the policy lifecycle are working. That is, conduct a pilot exercise.

Assuming the pilot is successful, other proposed policies can be sent through the processes of the policy lifecycle into production. Eventually, the enterprise should get into a steady state where most, or all, of the initially proposed policies have been operationalized. In the steady state, the Policy Portfolio becomes more of a tool for managing and reporting on data policies than as an initial list of required policies.

After implementing the initial set of policies, what should become of the Policy Portfolio? It could be treated simply as an artifact supporting an important one-time effort to operationalize the most needed data policies. However, an overall list of what data policies exist, what data policies are planned, and additional information about them will be needed. This is a serious requirement that we will discuss more in the chapter on policy metadata.

Suggestions for Initial Policy Portfolio

Table 9.1 below provides some suggestions for an initial portfolio of data policies. The suggested policies are grouped together as there may be a need for more than one policy to address a particular area. Of course, these are merely suggestions, and enterprises should follow the approach outlined above to come up with their own portfolio.

#	Policy	Description	Notes
1	**General Data Policies**		
1.1	Data Policy of Policies	Describes scope of data policies, who plays what role in their formulation, promulgation, compliance checking, and review. It also covers how data standards are developed and administered.	This has to be developed and approved before any other policy can be written.
1.2	Data Governance Policy	This describes the operating model for Data Governance, reporting lines, areas of responsibility, and DG roles and responsibilities.	This is often replaced by a Charter for the Data Governance unit.
1.3	Personal Data Handling Policy	Describes the general obligations that all staff have in handling data. For instance, for ensuring data quality during data entry. Usually, it is part of the new joiner's induction from Human Resources. Also includes how to get support.	This is a light policy as we cannot overload all staff in the enterprise. It is usually more focused on principles and introduces Data Governance as a support function.
1.4	End-user Computing Policy	All the important aspects of data governance and management have to be applied to End User Computing applications (EUCs), so this policy has to point them out. Also, the policy includes the need to register each EUC in a central inventory. The policy is often needed for compliance reasons (especially Key Person Risk).	A major need is for transparency to get people to divulge their EUC's. The enterprise definition of an EUC is important here, too, as it is part of a spectrum with models on the other end.

#	Policy	Description	Notes
1.5	Strategic Data Governance Project Engagement Policy	This describes how new IT projects, and pure business projects that involve data use or reuse, engage with Data Governance (DG). This is so that all DG needs are tackled early on and not discovered later when they cannot be remediated.	Without this policy, Data Governance is blind to what is happening with data on new projects.
1.6	Cloud / SaaS Data Management Policy	Describes how to deal with putting data into Cloud environments. Specifically, covers SaaS environments where SaaS providers may gain rights to enterprise metadata or even enterprise data. Also, covers the need to manage data assets in the Cloud to reduce storage and compute costs.	This is different from Third Part Data Sharing and Data Acquisition, which we cover later.
2	**Data Classification**		
2.1	Data Confidentiality Classification Policy	The core classification for business confidentiality, such as "confidential," "internal," and "public".	This policy is normally the responsibility of Information Security, not Data Governance. However, in some organizations it is Data Governance's responsibility.

#	Policy	Description	Notes
2.2	Data Classification for Compliance (excluding Confidentiality)	All other classifications needed for compliance (apart from business confidentiality) are gathered into this one policy. For instance, Personally Identifying Information (PII), Sensitive Personal Information (SPI), Personal Health Information (PHI), Personal Financial Information (PFI), etc. It includes how each classification is governed.	Since more and more classifications keep getting added, the policy may need to be high level and refer to a set of standards that deal with each classification. That is, a standard for PII, another standard for SPI, and so on.
3	**Data Acquisition**		
3.1	Data Vendor Policy	A policy for interacting with Data Vendors (entities that sell or license data to the enterprise). It ensures no "rogue" contracts can be signed with Data Vendors and that the enterprise will only deal with the ones it wants to. It also ensures the enterprise will have a 360 degree view of the vendor (especially for a "single invoice" per vendor that shows all costs).	This policy may require coordination with the Procurement department.

#	Policy	Description	Notes
3.2	Data Acquisition Policy	The steps needed to bring in datasets from (a) Data Vendors; (b) internal sources into (usually) a Data Lake. This is more than ingestion. It is the entire cycle from requirements to the first ingestion.	Roles and responsibilities are important here. A Data Acquisition Process or Lifecycle has to be laid out so people do not skip important checks. This policy helps protect the integrity of the Data Lake.
3.3	Internet Data Sourcing Policy	For screen scraping and "open source" dataset acquisition. It covers complying with source terms and conditions, respecting, for example, robots.txt, ensuring ping rates are not too high, etc. Also covers situations where consulting companies are hired to build datasets by sourcing data.	Screen scraping is easy to do with Python libraries and lots of tools. But most websites have Terms of Use that prohibit commercial reuse. This is a complex legal area. It must be dealt with carefully, and a policy is required to provide a clear framework.
3.4	Licensed Data Policy	This establishes a framework for how data that is under license from Data Vendors is dealt with. It is mainly about sharing this data within the enterprise and using licensed data from the vendors (figuring out what can be used within contractual limits). It also covers making sure contracts for data do not contain atypical clauses.	A major goal is to avoid contractual penalties with Data Vendors. The policy can be extended to charge back for usage within the enterprise, if this is desired.

#	Policy	Description	Notes
4	**Data Privacy and Retention**		
4.1	Data Privacy Policy	How to behave in terms of dealing with personal information. It is based on the principles of data privacy laws. The individual laws are dealt with in lower-level documents. Thus, the policy should include acceptable use of PII, though some organizations have a separate policy for acceptable use of PII.	The Data Privacy Policy is closely related to the Data Classification for Compliance Policy, as data has to be classified before applying any Data Privacy Policy.
4.2	Data Sharing with Third Parties Policy	This partly addresses how the enterprise shares data with service providers in the context of data privacy. But it also includes more general guidance on other aspects of data sharing with third parties, such as licensed data controls.	It might be thought that this could be included in the Data Privacy, but it covers all data shared with third parties, not just the Data Privacy aspects.
4.3	Data Sharing with Affiliates Policy	This is only needed if the enterprise has affiliated legal entities, such as if the enterprise is part of a group of companies. The policy provides guidance on how to share personal information in a way that is in compliance with data privacy laws. It is a bit specialized, hence has its own policy.	This policy is rather specialized and may only be needed in a legal entity that operates in a jurisdiction with a Data Privacy law that covers affiliates.

#	Policy	Description	Notes
4.4	Data Retention Policy	The framework for understanding when data should be permanently disposed of (by anonymization or deletion), and the ability to deal with legal holds. Proof of disposal is also covered. Archiving should also be covered in this policy.	There may be a Records Management Group in the enterprise that manages this policy. If not, then Data Governance must manage it.
4.5	Internet Translation Service Policy	This limits the usage of some Internet translation services. Some services capture all text entered and index it. The policy is needed to prevent loss of intellectual property, PII, licensed data, etc.	It may be possible to simply limit access to these sites. That is a question for Information Security.
4.6	Open AI Data Use Policy	This is similar to the Internet Translation Service Policy. Staff are increasingly using public open AI services, and must be prevented from inputting confidential or sensitive data as they prompt these services.	It may be possible to simply limit access to these sites. If this approach is taken, then Information Security should create the policy.

5	**Internal Data Sharing**		
5.1	Internal Data Sharing Policy	This policy covers how data is shared among teams. This will involve data sharing agreements (which are specified in standards) and producer/consumer responsibilities. The need to register data sharing is covered. The policy should aim to get documentation created that will provide lineage at a business dataset level.	If the concept of Data Products turns out to be durable, this policy can address their needs also.

6	**Data Anonymization / Deidentification**		
6.1	Data Deidentification Policy	What data under what circumstances needs to be deidentified. This generally covers production data used for testing, but can also be applied to additional needs.	The policy is closely related to the Data Classification for Compliance Policy, as data has to be classified to identify what needs to be anonymized.
6.2	Data Encryption Policy	Data at rest and data in motion that needs to be encrypted are covered by this policy. The kind of data to encrypt and general methods for encryption are specified. Pseudonymization is often covered in a Data Privacy Policy, but can be covered here instead.	It is preferable to have just one policy to deal with encryption. Unfortunately, this is a topic that often gets added to other policies that are not specifically about data.

7	**Unstructured Data**		
7.1	Unstructured Data Stores Policy	This policy outlines the rights and responsibilities of staff who create unstructured data stores, like SharePoint and OneDrive. The staff who do this must add them to a central inventory of unstructured data stores, describe what level of sensitive data to be stored there, and identify individuals responsible for the store (key person risk is important here). Note that this is an inventory of all unstructured data stores and not the files in each one.	Of particular interest is the sensitivity classification of the entire data store. The policy must have a definition of what "unstructured" means.
7.2	Unstructured Data Assets Policy	This applies to the files located in each unstructured data store. It covers how a file-level inventory will be built for each store via automation and the rules for classifying files for sensitivity and retention (at a minimum).	The two policies described earlier for Data Classification were intended for structured data. Thus, the classification of unstructured data assets will need to be addressed in this policy.

8	**Data Quality**		
8.1	Data Quality Production Monitoring Policy	This describes the minimum Data Quality (DQ) monitoring required for production environments. It covers (a) data entry quality assurance; (b) profiling of data to detect outliers; (c) Data Quality Business Rules specification, curation, and operationalization; (d) handling DQ event detection and notifications; (e) Reporting on data health and data quality.	This policy will need to link to many lower-level standards and processes.
8.2	Data Quality Testing Policy	This describes the testing required in data-centric development projects to ensure data quality. It describes the kind of testing to be carried out, such as the reconciliation of source to target.	There is a possibility that Information Technology (IT) already has this in a policy.
8.3	Data Issue Management Policy	This policy describes the overall framework for arriving at a resolution for data issues detected in production. It includes logging the resolution so it is available for reuse if the problem occurs again.	Standards for best practices will also be needed.

9	Master and Reference Data		
9.1	Reference Data Policy	Defines the scope of Reference Data (code tables). Distinguishes between External and Internal Reference Data. The former requires a subscription to an authority. The latter requires complete governance within the enterprise. The minimum set of management tasks for Reference Data are described. The roles and responsibilities are outlined.	Reference Data is important but poorly governed in most enterprises. The policy will improve the situation.
9.2	Master Data Policy	Master Data is defined, and the Master Data Entities managed by the enterprise are enumerated. The constraints on systems creating Master Data versus sourcing it from a central location are described. The ideal architectural options for the enterprise, such as centralized, coexistence, or consolidated, are specified. The strategy and goals for Master Data are explained.	The policy will be general in nature since different Master Data entities, such as Customer and Product, have different detailed management needs.

10	**Data Architecture and Modeling**		
10.1	Data Architecture Policy	This policy includes a set of Data Architecture principles that need to be followed in the enterprise. It also includes a framework for architecture diagrams and where to store architectural metadata.	The Enterprise Architecture function should be accountable in this area, and may already have such a policy. If there is no Enterprise Architecture function, then Data Governance may need to be accountable for the policy.
10.2	Data Modeling Policy	A framework for how to do data modeling and when models are required. It specifies how data modeling aligns with Data Architecture and Data Governance. The governance of data modeling standards, such as naming conventions, is explained.	The Enterprise Architecture function should be accountable in this area, and may already have such a policy. If there is no Enterprise Architecture function, then Data Governance may need to be accountable for the policy.

11	Semantics		
11.1	Critical Data Elements (CDE's) Policy	Such a policy is needed in many financial services companies for compliance reasons. The criteria for identifying CDE's are either described or the process for specifying the criteria is described. How CDE's are inventoried is described. The roles and responsibilities for CDEs are described. The special care given to CDE's is described, such as the curation of definitions, data quality standards, and support. CDE's can also be a ranking of data elements for Data Governance attention and focus.	Make sure this policy is needed before writing it.
11.2	Business Terms and Data Elements Policy	This policy focuses on new business terms and data elements, rather than the existing ones (though they can be covered if needed). If, in new projects, new business terms and/or data elements are created, then the business analyst involved has to put them in the correct business glossary (often in a data catalog). Minimum quality standards for content are outlined.	This policy has to be coupled with details about the processes for doing this work.

11.3	Reports Management Policy	This policy specifies the report lifecycle. The need to add each report to an inventory with owners, users, etc., is described. The need to track distribution is generally reserved for very important reports. Annual reconfirmation of the fact that the report is still in use is covered. Report certification is also dealt with, if needed.	This policy may be required for compliance reasons.
12	**Data Science / Machine Learning (ML) / Artificial Intelligence (AI)**		
12.1	Data Ethics Policy	A Data Ethics Board may sometimes be needed to discuss questions about the ethical use of data, including in ML and AI projects. If so, this policy covers it. Sometimes, the Board must drive this effort for compliance reasons, or to prove that a company is serious about these matters.	This is now being combined with an AI policy in many enterprises.

12.2	Data Usage for Machine Learning (ML) Policy	This policy will cover any special aspects of data handling for how ML. Feature engineering and hyperparameters are dealt with. Synthetic data for testing and training is also covered. These are very ML- and Data Science-specific areas. The policy does not replicate what other policies have. Ensuring data does not lead to bias or disparate impact is important, but may require working with the Data Ethics Board. Model Maintenance and retraining are also covered, as is establishing a Model Inventory.	This is a difficult area since it overlaps Data Governance and Model Governance, which can be different organizational units. It is not clear how Model Governance is operationalized in many enterprises. Some companies merge Data and Model Governance, but Model Governance is, at least in theory, a distinct area.
12.3	Data Usage for AI Policy	This policy deals with the specifics of data management for AI. Since nothing can easily be deleted from AI after training, the detection of PII and confidential information before it goes into AI is very important. There are other data handling needs, too, like profanity detection and validation of quality of sources. AI is an emerging policy area.	Since AI is emerging, special attention should be given to it. New or modified policies are likely to be needed as the technology advances.

Table 9.1: Suggestions for an Initial Data Policy Portfolio

## Chapter 10

Policy Metadata

In the previous chapter, we discussed the Policy Portfolio, which structurally is going to be a fairly simple list of policies. This list is metadata, and metadata is usually defined as:

---

data about data

However, this definition does not convey a lot of information. Furthermore, the Policy Portfolio is not really "data about data." It is a list of policies. A better definition of "metadata" is needed.

We define metadata as:
the information needed to understand and manage
the information assets of the enterprise

This definition of "metadata" includes both structured and unstructured metadata, where structured metadata is the kind that can be represented as rows and columns, and unstructured is pure text, image, video, audio, or something similar.

We will only consider structured metadata for policies, as this has the most management requirements for Data Governance units today.

Basic Structure of the Policy Portfolio

Data Governance will need to design the table that is the Policy Portfolio. Table 10.1 provides a design for a simple Policy Portfolio Table that can track individual data policies.

Column Name	Column Description	Datatype
Policy Name	The official name of the policy. This must be unique, meaning no two policies can have the same name. Must be entered.	Text
Current Policy Status	One of: Planned, Current, Discontinued. These are the three basic states of a policy. Must be entered.	Single Selection
Initial Effective Date	The date on which the policy first came into force. Do not enter for policies in "Planned" status. Must be entered for policies in "Current" or "Discontinued" state.	Date

Column Name	Column Description	Datatype
Last Reviewed Date	The date on which the policy was last reviewed for changes. Must be entered for policies in "Current" or "Discontinued" state.	Date
Current Version Effective Date	The date on which the current version of the policy first came into force. Do not enter for policies in "Planned" status. Must be entered for policies in "Current" or "Discontinued" state.	Date
Current Version Number	The number of the current version. Do not enter for policies in "Planned" status. Must be entered for policies in "Current" or "Discontinued" state.	Text
Discontinuation Date	The date on which the policy was discontinued. Mandatory for policies in "Discontinued" state. Must not be entered for policies in "Planned" or "Current" state.	Date
Policy Administrator	The name of the individual who is the Policy Administrator for the policy. See Chapter 13 for more details of this role. Must be entered.	Text

Table 10.1: Basic Design of the Policy Portfolio Table

This design has the Policy Name as the field that uniquely identifies a policy record. If it felt that the Policy Name can change after the policy is implemented, then a different field will be needed. However, changing a Policy Name after implementation can cause a lot of confusion across the enterprise and is not a good idea. An alternate field that provides uniqueness, if really needed, could be something like a simple sequence number.

We will discuss the Policy Administrator in subsequent chapters. From the design point of view, the column for Policy Administrator could be a simple text field or a relation to a separate Person table. The latter allows for a more robust design for metadata in general beyond the Policy Portfolio, but is more complex.

Implementing the Policy Portfolio Table

We now have a design for a basic Policy Portfolio Table, but how should it be implemented? Because the Policy Portfolio Table looks like a simple list, it is tempting to implement it as a spreadsheet, like Excel. Many other data governance concerns are equally simple lists, so spreadsheets seem the easiest way to go in general. This is what we usually see in practice.

Unfortunately, the initial appearance of simplicity may be misleading. Data policies may be related to specific data management areas, different parts of the business, be related to different categories of data, and so on. There will likely be different ways of categorizing policies themselves. There may be "families" of policies, different policies will be at different stages in the policy lifecycle, some policies may be more important than others, and so on. Thus, while a list of policies is simple, there can be a web of relationships with other "simple" tables.

This brings us to the consideration of data catalogs.

> *Today, many Data Governance units have purchased data catalogs, which manage a great deal of metadata that Data Governance needs to do its work.*

Data catalogs are usually configurable, meaning that we can create the equivalent of database tables within them simply through their user interface. This certainly makes the task of implementing a table structure like that shown in Table 10.1 easy. More importantly, the table can be related to tables of other metadata in the data catalog. This is a very important point.

Figure 10.1 illustrates how a data catalog can have a Policy Table (the Policy Portfolio) and how it relates to other metadata tables.

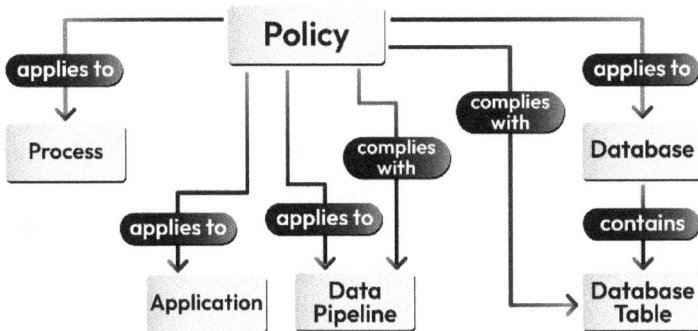

Figure 10.1: Illustration of How a Data Catalog Can Relate Policy Information to Other Information about Data

The ability of a data catalog to manage these relationships opens up the possibility of capturing information about what data assets a policy governs and whether these assets are in compliance with the policy. Given that so many Data Governance units have data catalogs already, it is logical to house the Policy Portfolio in them.

> *If a Data Governance unit does not have a data catalog yet finds an Excel spreadsheet too limiting, an alternative is to use one of the SaaS software products that are simple relational databases.*

These products are platforms where end users can easily create database tables and workflows to manage information in a collaborative environment. Given the rather simple structure of a Policy Portfolio, they are a good fit for this application.

Metadata for Managing the Policy Lifecycle

Table 10.1 provides an example of the basic metadata to manage the Policy Portfolio. However, if there is a desire to manage the policy lifecycle for each policy, then the design needs to be updated. Table 10.2 shows additional columns corresponding to parts of the policy lifecycle, which we will discuss in more detail in subsequent chapters.

Column Name	Column Description	Datatype
Request Received Date	The date on which the request to create, update, or discontinue this policy was received.	Date
Formulation Start Date	The date on which policy formulation began for the policy. Leave empty if it has not begun yet.	Date
Harmonization Start Date	The date on which policy harmonization began for the policy. Leave empty if it has not begun yet.	Date
Promulgation Start Date	The date on which promulgation activities began for the policy. Leave empty if it has not begun yet.	Date
Approval Start Date	The date on which policy approval activities began for the policy. Leave empty if it has not begun yet.	Date
Approval End Date	The date on which the final approval for the policy was granted. Leave empty if it has not happened yet.	Date
Promulgation Start Date	The date on which promulgation activities began for the policy. Leave empty if it has not begun yet.	Date
Previous Review Date	The date on which the previous annual review of the policy was carried out. Leave empty if no previous review has occurred.	Date

Column Name	Column Description	Datatype
Next Review Date	The date on which the next review of the policy will occur. Leave empty if the policy has been discontinued.	Date

Table 10.2: Possible Additional Data Fields for Policy Portfolio Table

The additional columns shown in Table 10.2 allow reporting to be done when a particular policy has passed through a particular phase of the policy lifecycle. The Next Review Date allows scheduling of the next annual policy review, which we shall discuss in a subsequent chapter.

There is both a start date and end date for policy approval. This is because we need to know both when the approval phase started and when all approvals have been received for the policy, given that there may be multiple approvals.

With these columns, it is possible to see where a policy is in the policy lifecycle and to understand when a policy was in a prior phase. Of course, there is no need to have these additional columns if there is no desire to track or report on the progress of a data policy through the policy lifecycle.

Metadata for Efficiency Reporting

If there is a desire to report on the efficiency with which policies move through the policy lifecycle, then we will need planned and actual dates, rather than just the actual dates shown in Table 10.2. Table 10.3 illustrates this for the policy formulation dates.

Column Name	Column Description	Datatype
Formulation Initial Planned Start Date	The date on which policy formulation was first planned to start for the policy. Do not update if the planned start date gets changed.	Date
Formulation Actual Start Date	The date on which policy formulation actually began for the policy. Leave empty if it has not begun yet.	Date
Formulation Actual End Date	The date on which policy formulation ended began for the policy. Leave empty if it has not ended yet.	Date

Table 10.3: More Detailed Date Fields for Policy Formulation

This approach of having three date fields applies to policy formulation, policy harmonization, policy promulgation, and policy approval. In this way, it is possible to calculate the time between the original plan for the policy to start in the lifecycle phase and when that phase was actually started and completed. This can give an idea of how efficient the policy processes are. It can also highlight the need for more resources.

Again, there is no point in having these columns if there is no interest in reporting on the efficiency of the policy processes.

Obviously, there are alternate designs that involve multiple tables to capture events at a more granular level and workflows that are not linear but involve going back to an earlier phase. Enterprises should consider these alternate designs if they support specific requirements.

Expanded Policy Metadata

So far, we have been focused on metadata for the Policy Portfolio. However, as shown in Figure 10.1 with the use of a data catalog, many possibilities are opened in terms of how policy metadata can be related to other metadata. It is important not to start by solutioning these possibilities, but to capture the actual use cases that involve policy metadata. Once these are understood, we can create the metadata designs for the data catalog. The use cases have to involve the production of one or more specific outputs that are then used for a purpose.

We should not construct complex metadata configurations just because we can or because we feel they might be useful in some way.

This creates unnecessary complexity and is a waste of resources.

We cannot cover the full range of possibilities here, so each enterprise must build its own metadata architecture for policies, depending on its needs. However, we will discuss core metadata requirements of the individual phases of the policy lifecycle in subsequent chapters.

## Chapter 11

Taking Over Data Policies

We must consider the current state of the enterprise at the outset of data policy work. There is almost certain to be an existing array of policies dealing with data management to some extent. What do we do with these policies? The policy of policies gives authority to develop data policies to Data Governance with oversight from the Data Policy Oversight Committee. Does this mean that the existing policies are automatically transferred to Data Governance, do things remain the same, or is there some other solution?

The first thing to do is to find out what exists.

Current State Assessment

A current state assessment should be undertaken by Data Governance to find all existing policies and identify any content about data in them. This represents the current data policy content that Data Governance should, in theory, take over.

Such an exercise can sometimes be more difficult than it seems. Generally, enterprise-wide policies are listed prominently and easy to find on the corporate intranet. But sometimes, they are not listed this way, and there may be departmental policies that are even less easily discoverable. This may seem improbable, but it does happen. Let us for a moment put ourselves in the position of a Data Governance unit trying to carry out this task.

Our Data Governance unit should build a list of all active policies in the enterprise based on whatever research it can do, and then circulate this among department heads to find out if there are any additional policies that the department heads know of. If there are any such policies, they are added to the list. Of course, this presupposes that the department heads have already received communications about what Data Governance is and its role in the enterprise.

After we complete the list, the next task is to find the latest version of each policy in the list. Again, this might seem easy, but it can sometimes be quite difficult. If the author of the policy is identifiable, we can contact them to confirm the location of the latest version. If this is not possible, compliance functions that work with the policy, like Internal Audit, can be asked to provide the confirmation.

The fact that confirmation has been obtained, together with the location of the latest version, can be added to the list of active enterprise policies.

Policy Review

Once we locate the latest versions of all active policies, Data Governance staff can read through them or simply search for any mention of data. Perhaps there will not be many existing policies that are truly data policies, but there are quite likely to be mentions of data in some.

The order in which the policies are processed may help the overall effort. The shortest and least complex policies can be tackled first, and the more complex and longer ones later on. This will give Data Governance staff a better chance to learn about the content of the policies.

If any mention of data is found, then it needs to be recorded. This requires yet another list where the policy name, the section, page, paragraph, and line where the mention begins are captured, along with the full citation where data is mentioned. Let us call this the Policy Citation List. Of course, if an entire policy is about data, there is no need to copy the citations. The policy itself can simply be listed as being wholly relevant.

Policy Analysis

The analysis can begin after collecting all of the data-related citations. We should establish a method for doing the analysis, such as:

- **Step 1 - Identify Existing Data Policies**: In this step, we identify all policies that primarily deal with data management. These are any policies intended to deal with data management, rather than being policies for something else with some elements of data management contained in them. We must also identify the organizational units accountable for the policies. Not all policies that are explicitly data policies may be recognizable from their titles. They need to be read. The remaining policies are not explicitly about data management but may still have elements concerning data management.

- **Step 2 - Identify Relevant Citations:** Looking at the citations in the remaining policies that are not purely data policies, we decide whether they are material to data governance and data management, or incidental and only support concerns that have nothing to do with data governance and data management. The Policy Citation List can be marked up to identify the relevant citations. Irrelevant citations need not be processed further.

- **Step 3 - Identify any inconsistencies.** We must identify any citations in the same or different policies that are inconsistent or contradict each other. We cannot process these citations further at this point. We will discuss them more in the chapter on policy harmonization.

Once we complete the analysis, policy transfers to Data Governance can occur, at least in theory. Figure 11.1 illustrates the analysis we have just described.

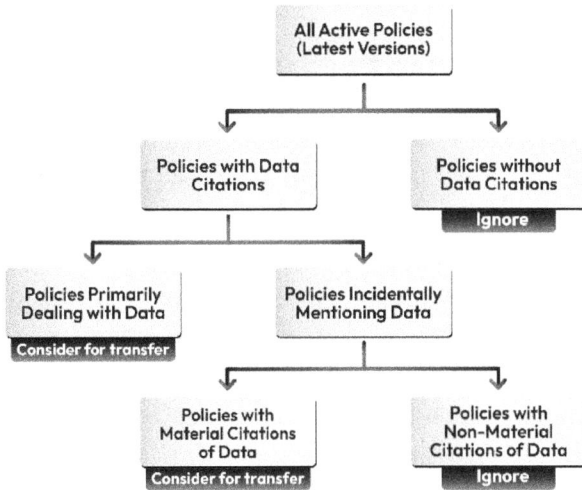

Figure 11.1: Illustration of Policy Analysis

Whole Policies and Partner Organizations

Data Governance can do all the discovery and analysis work described in this chapter before the policy of policies has been put into effect. There is no need to get approval from the Data Policy Oversight Committee, which, in any case, has not been formed yet. On the other hand, some organizations may feel it is better to wait until after the policy of policies is adopted before asking any units outside of Data Governance for their inputs, because an explanation has to be provided about why this information is being requested.

> *However, only after the policy of policies is in force can Data Governance request any other organizational unit transfer data policies in whole or part to Data Governance. Only then will Data Governance have the required authority.*

It is probably best to start with the existing data policies–the ones that are wholly or almost wholly about data governance and data management. Data Governance must go to the organizational units responsible for these policies and negotiate the future of them. For instance, the Information Security unit will likely develop a Data Confidentiality Classification Policy rather than Data Governance. This is as it should be since Information Security is mandated to protect the data and system resources of the enterprise, and it has the technical skills to do this.

It will very likely be that in all enterprises, some specialized centralized administrative units genuinely need to develop and implement policies largely about data. These policies have to remain with the specialized units involved.

The way for a Data Governance unit to deal with this situation is first to identify all these specialized "horizontal" units (so-called because their remit spans the entire enterprise) and then approach them to discuss who does what in terms of governing data, including policy work. The ideal outcome of these discussions is a Memorandum of Understanding (MoU) that specifies in writing the relationship between Data Governance and the specialized unit. The MoU must include who is responsible for what policies. If the specialized unit is responsible for any data-related policy, then the MoU must specify that Data Governance is consulted about such policies and that the specialized unit uses Data Governance's standards for data policy work.

The other units are often only too happy for this assistance from Data Governance. In particular, they are very interested in Data Governance's capabilities for promulgating policies. This is often because the other units often lack strong communication capabilities, which are typically well-developed in Data Governance units. In such cases, these other units may ask Data Governance to partner with them to promulgate their policies.

Units that refuse to transfer a policy to Data Governance are dealt with later in this chapter.

Figure 11.2 illustrates these different courses of action.

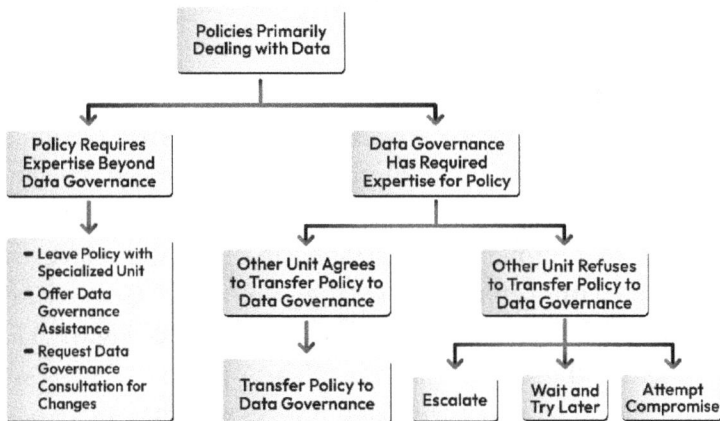

Figure 11.2: Illustration of Options in Data Governance Taking Over Whole Policies

This leaves data policies that really should be taken over by Data Governance. If the currently accountable organizational unit does not have materially greater expertise than Data Governance, then Data Governance must insist that the policy be transferred to Data Governance. This does not mean that the policy has to change immediately; it simply means that Data Governance is taking it over.

Citation-Level Transfer

The remaining policies are not whole policies addressing data governance or data management concerns, but simply have citations that Data Governance needs to take over. We have to remove the citations from the policies in their current locations and move them to new policies developed by Data Governance. As a reminder, we have already discussed that these citations are materially relevant to data governance and data management. As such, they need to be transferred to the Data Governance unit.

The transfer of citations is somewhat complex. Data Governance needs to develop new policies that contain these citations. At the same time, the organizational unit accountable for the original policies has to update their policies to remove the citations, or perhaps replace the citations with references to the new Data Governance policy. These actions have to be coordinated. Figure 11.3 illustrates these alternatives. This means that Data Governance has to formulate policy requests (see next chapter) to create the new policies into which the citations will be transferred. These policy requests will likely be among the first that Data Governance will generate. It is very important to follow the steps of the processes specified for the policy lifecycle and not to ignore them.

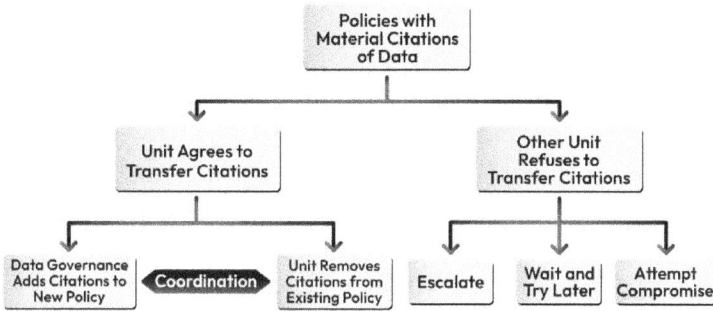

Figure 11.3: Illustration of How Material Citations Can Be Handled

One further point is that the citations do not have to be copied verbatim into the new policies. They can be reformulated to use more consistent terminology and better fit within the context of the new policies.

Involvement of the Data Policy Oversight Committee

The level of work required to transfer to Data Governance whole data policies and citations about data in other policies is very high. It also involves working with a large number of other units across the enterprise, at least potentially. It is, therefore, a good idea to formulate the work as a project and bring it to the Data Policy Oversight Committee for approval.

There are two benefits to this approach:

- The project will have the backing of a major policy-related committee, which can help motivate the other organizational units to cooperate.

- The members of the committee, especially those from outside Data Governance, may be able to offer advice on how to approach the other units, and may even be prepared to help.

The committee should be involved after the discovery and analysis work has been completed and a project plan developed. All the information required by the committee should then be available.

With respect to Data Governance, the Data Policy Operations Committee should coordinate the discovery, analysis, project formulation, and project planning. This will help make sure that nothing has been missed. A formal request to the Data Policy Oversight Committee from the Data Policy Operationalization Committee will give the project an additional level of institutional importance, which can only help deal with the other parts of the organization with policies covering data.

Traceability of Policies and Citations

The transfer of whole policies to the control of Data Governance, and the transfer of citations from old policies not under the control of Data Governance to new policies under the control of Data Governance should be tracked to allow for future audits.

This is probably best done using the Policy Citation List.

Once the project finishes and all transfers complete, we can retain the Policy Citation List for any future reference. This is most likely to be needed for auditors and regulators. Such a large-scale revision of policies will undoubtedly attract their attention.

Dealing with Uncooperative Units

Data Governance should not approach other units out of the blue and demand they relinquish control of entire policies and policy citations to Data Governance. Rather, Data Governance should first execute a communications strategy so these other units know what Data Governance is, what its remit is, and where it is located in the organization.

Even then, Data Governance needs to craft its message about policy transfers before approaching any other organizational unit and be prepared to handle objections in a diplomatic manner.

It is not necessary to come to a meeting of minds in a single meeting. Discussions can be held in one meeting so that Data Governance can present its case without requiring a response from the other organizational unit. The decision to accept Data Governance's proposal (or not) can be addressed in a subsequent meeting.

If an organizational unit does not want to transfer policies and/or citations that Data Governance feels it should, then Data Governance will likely have to raise this issue to the

Data Policy Oversight Committee. In these kinds of situations, compromises that are less than ideal may be the only real option. Getting executives involved is not a good idea, as executives typically dislike issues being escalated to them. Executives want issues solved at a lower level. In such circumstances, Data Governance may be wise to compromise but ask to be consulted about data-related policies that an organizational unit is unwilling to transfer. Over the long run, Data Governance can wait until there is personnel turnover or the other units get more comfortable working with Data Governance, and then try again to take over the policies.

## Chapter 12

Policy Requests

At this point, we have reviewed how to start data policy work. We will now go through the policy lifecycle phase by phase. We will consider the governance and management needs, and also implications for the policy of policies.

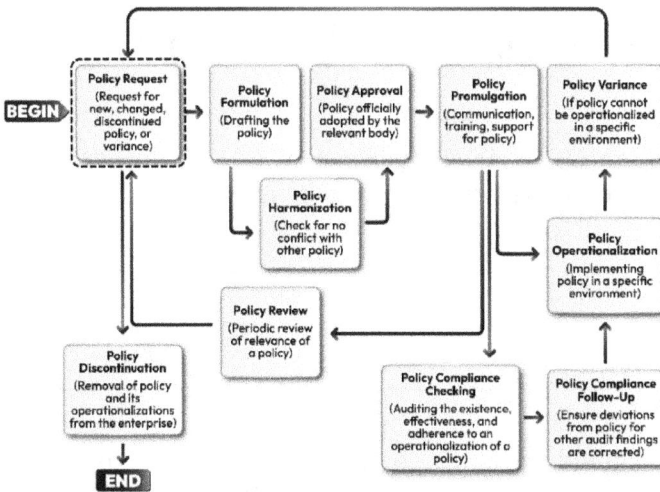

Figure 12.1: Location of Policy Requests in the Policy Lifecycle

The first phase of the data policy lifecycle is policy requests.

A policy request is a request to initiate an action on a data policy. The possible types of requests are:

- **New:** A request for a new policy.

- **Review:** A request to formally review a policy, with the possibility of changing or discontinuing the policy.

- **Change:** A request for a change to a policy. This may or may not be as a result of a review.

- **Variance:** A request from an area of the enterprise to be exempted from all or part of a policy.

- **Discontinuation:** A request to eliminate a policy, possibly with it being replaced by another policy. This may or may not be as a result of a review.

Why Manage Policy Requests Formally?

Managing policy requests formally might seem to introduce unnecessary work, perhaps even be overly bureaucratic. However, there are some good reasons for it.

> *The first is fairness. Anyone in the enterprise should be able to make a data policy request for any reason.*

This should be their right and it should not be questioned. The policy request will be evaluated and may be rejected.

At the outset, Data Governance may have to initiate the first data policies, as we have discussed previously. However, in a steady state, the possibility of making a policy request should be open to all.

We need to avoid a non-transparent and frankly undemocratic process where a particular unit, like Data Governance, makes policy requests in a completely different way than anyone else in the enterprise and gets special treatment, like prioritization of their requests. Even worse is a situation where, outside of Data Governance, nobody is aware that they are allowed to make policy requests. In such circumstances, staff will feel that data policies are being pushed on them without even the possibility of consultation, leading to resentment and difficulties in getting data policy adoption. Remember that data is everywhere in the enterprise, so data policies will impact almost everyone.

Of course, Data Governance is the unit with the deepest expertise in data matters, so it is likely to generate the largest number of policy requests. It will also be the unit that is most aware of legal and regulatory needs concerning data (along with Risk and Legal) that may require policies. But Data Governance cannot be aware of all the data policy needs across the enterprise, so staff must be allowed to submit policy requests to deal with situations that affect them.

A second reason is that formal data policy request management enables Data Governance to track and measure its work. By forcing formalization, there is recordkeeping of policy requests, from which reports can show such things as the number of requests, the time taken to service them, triage levels, and so on. This proves that Data Governance is doing its policy work in an efficient, effective, and well-governed manner.

A third reason is traceability, especially if Data Governance gets audited. Each policy action, like developing a new policy or updating an existing one, can be traced back to a request from a particular individual or organizational unit. How each request was processed can be clearly demonstrated.

By contrast, if policy requests are simply treated informally, it will not be possible to report much on them or provide uniform documentary evidence of how they were processed.

It should always be remembered that governance in all its forms – including data governance – requires showing how things were done and proving that they were done in the correct manner.

Therefore, formal management of policy requests is highly recommended.

Policy Request Log

A Policy Request Log is needed to formally manage policy requests. information on all policy requests is recorded here to better manage them.

We have already discussed policy metadata with a focus on the Policy Portfolio. The Policy Request Log is another fairly simple list. It can be an Excel spreadsheet, a Google Sheet, a configuration in a data catalog, or a SaaS software with similar functionality for maintaining simple lists. The same points from the chapter on policy metadata apply to the Policy Request Log.

One individual from the Data Governance unit will need to be assigned to manage the Policy Request Log. We will call this role the Policy Registrar. There should also be a backup person for when the Policy Registrar is absent.

A possible design for the columns in the Policy Request Log appears in Table 12.1.

Item	Column	Description
1	Data Policy Request Id	A unique identifier assigned to each policy request that is received. For example, a sequence number, or an intelligent key like date in YYYMMDD format and a sequence number within that, for example, "2027100501."
2	Data Policy Original Request	The content of the request, as it originally came in. This must be complete and must not be changed.
3	Requestor Name	The name of the individual who made the request. This is the author of the request, and may be different from the person who initiated the request.
4	Requestor Organizational Unit	The name of the organizational unit that the requestor works in.
5	Type of Request	One of: New, Review, Change, Variance, Discontinuation, Other.
6	Date Request Received	The date the request was received.

Item	Column	Description
7	Request Channel	The primary channel through which the request was received, such as email, document, verbal, or other. By "primary," we mean the place where it was originally documented. For instance, a request can be in a document like an audit finding, which is then emailed to Data Governance. The primary channel is the document, not the email.
8	Request Reference	Whatever uniquely identifies the request. It could be a date/time/subject of an email, a file name of a document, or a link to a document. This provides an audit trail and allows us to refer to the original request later in the policy lifecycle.
9	Initial Request Decision	One of: Not a Policy Request, Duplicate Request, Referred to Data Policy Oversight Committee.
10	Initial Request Decision Date	The date on which the Request Initial Decision was made.
11	Initial Request Decision Rationale	The reason for the Initial Request Decision.
12	Policy Oversight Committee Decision	One of: Approve, Deny, More Information Required, On Hold.
13	Policy Oversight Committee Decision	The date on which the Policy Oversight Committee Decision was made.
14	Policy Oversight Committee Decision Rationale	The reason for the Policy Oversight Committee Decision.

Table 12.1: Possible Design of the Policy Request Log

Policy Requests from Outside Data Governance

Data Governance should ideally have a general email address that anyone in the enterprise can email for any reason. Dedicated personnel in Data Governance should review the inbox for this email account.

If an email appears to be for a policy request, it must be forwarded to the Policy Registrar. The Policy Registrar will then review the email and triage it. The initial triage is:

- The email is clearly a policy request.
- The email is clearly not a policy request.
- It is not clear if the email is a policy request.

If it is not clear that the email is a policy request, then the Policy Registrar must contact the sender and ask for clarification. This process should continue until it becomes clear to the Policy Registrar that there is or is not a policy request.

If the email is clearly not a policy request, triage it further as follows:

- The email is not policy related.
- The email is policy related, but is not a policy request.
- It is unclear if the email is policy-related or not.

As before, if it is unclear that the email is policy related, the Policy Registrar must contact the sender and find out if the email has anything to do with policies. If the email has nothing to do with policies, the Policy Registrar should try to put the sender in touch with whatever area is most relevant, like the IT Help Desk, although the Policy Registrar may not always be certain of the area.

If the email is about policies, although not a request, the Policy Registrar should try to answer the inquiry or, failing that, put the sender in touch with whoever is accountable for the data policy the sender is inquiring about.

This leaves the situation where the email is actually a policy request. The further triage here is:

- It is a new request, that is, for something that was never requested before.
- It is a request for something that was processed in the past, and all actions are complete.
- It is a request for something that is currently being processed.

If the email was a request that was processed in the past or is currently being processed, the Policy Registrar must inform the sender of this, and no further action is required.

To do this, the Policy Registrar will need to consult the Policy Portfolio. Perhaps a similar request was considered in the past but was denied. Or perhaps a similar request is currently being processed.

If the email is a request for something new, the Policy Registrar must ensure there is enough information to move forward with consideration of the request. Additional details may be needed from the requestor to do this.

Every policy request is captured in the Policy Request Log. The Type of Request may not be initially clear, which is why there is an "Other" option. If the request is eventually determined not to be a policy request as a result of the triages, then the Type of Request remains "Other". Only if the request is for something that is new and policy-related does it move forward for consideration by the Data Policy Oversight Committee.

When the Policy Registrar is certain that the new request is sufficiently well documented, the Policy Registrar can change the Initial Request Decision to "Referred to Data Policy Oversight Committee." If the policy request is not new, then the Initial Request Decision is set to one of the other values and is not considered further.

The Policy Registrar makes the decision at this point as it only requires simple triages. A rationale must also be documented for the decision.

Figure 12.2 summarizes the initial processing of a policy request.

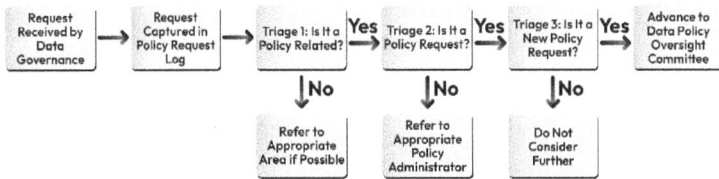

Figure 12.2: Summary of Initial Processing of a Policy Request

From an administrative perspective, every email received should be acknowledged within 24 hours. Analysis of the email should be completed within a timeframe set by Data Governance, such as three business days. The final decision regarding the email must be clearly communicated, with reasoning provided. If the request is to be referred to the Data Policy Oversight Committee, the requester should be informed as to what to expect in the future. If the policy request is not referred to the Data Policy Oversight Committee, there needs to be an escalation mechanism if the requester disagrees. For instance, the requester could be informed that they could make their case to the Data Policy Operations Committee.

At this point, the intake process for policy requests is completed.

If data policy requests from outside Data Governance are to be encouraged, then the general staff of the enterprise needs to be informed of this option and how to use it. Data Governance must develop communication measures to do this. We will review communications more in the chapter on policy promulgation.

Policy Requests from Inside Data Governance

Many new policy requests will come from within Data Governance. These will include requests for the initial policies that were added to the policy portfolio and actions arising from policy reviews.

Additionally, Data Governance should be aware of any changes in the regulatory environment that will require new policies. For instance, this was the case a number of years ago when data privacy became important due to new laws in many jurisdictions. Similarly, business changes, such as moving into certain industries like consumer finance, can also require new data policies.

Data Governance needs to build the capacity to do this kind of monitoring. Keeping up with the published business strategy of the enterprise will help, as will keeping up to date with developments in the data industry. We have already discussed creating strong relationships with areas like Legal and Regulatory Reporting, which will also help in this regard.

As Data Governance identifies needs for new or changed policies, it will create new policy requests and send them to the Policy Registrar, who will process them as described above.

Policy Gap Analysis

There is another very important way in which Data Governance should generate new policy requests.

> *It is a core task of Data Governance to understand the data management practices that are in place across the enterprise.*

This is not easy to do, as it is about how staff behave with respect to data. For instance, in a particular system, staff may start using certain data entry fields that have not been used much in the past to capture information these fields were not intended to capture. Furthermore, the staff involved may not tell anyone else, but the data involved may flow to many other databases. Eventually, these downstream databases may be negatively impacted by the field reuse in the source system.

This is an example of poor data management behavior. Data Governance needs to identify these kinds of situations and determine what the appropriate data management state should be. If the gap between the current state and the appropriate state is sufficiently large, then a policy is likely needed. The appropriate state does not have to be an ideal state that may be impossible to attain. However, it must align with the overall data principles developed for data governance and management.

The main difficulty here is that Data Governance needs to determine what data management practices are happening across the enterprise. At least initially, this is not technical and Data Governance does not have to do things like inspect databases or reverse engineer data flows. So, how can Data Governance identify policy gaps? Here are some approaches:

- Data Governance can gather intelligence from centralized units like Internal Audit, Legal, and IT who may see data issues in areas of the enterprise they work with. Perhaps they see too much variability in the ways that data management tasks are carried out across the enterprise.

- If Data Governance has established a network of Data Stewards across the enterprise, they can be trained to be sensitive to any data management needs and issues in their areas and bring that information back to Data Governance.

- Data Governance can assess data management practices in particular business units. These exercises could be combined with activities like providing data literacy training, so they do not look too much like audits.

- Data Governance can select themes like data privacy or data quality and do assessments focused on these themes across the enterprise. This differs from the previous point in that Data Governance has a particular focus. Automated surveys may be of assistance in this approach, given that it is so specific.

Clearly, Data Governance needs some kind of strategy for the long term in order to identify policy gaps. At the outset, Data Governance may be concerned with building the organizational framework, implementing metadata management technologies, and developing procedures for policies. However, after a while, these will be in place and Data Governance can focus on the steady state.

The Data Policy Operations Committee should develop a long-term strategy for finding policy gaps and initiating policy requests to fill them. This strategy should be submitted to the Data Policy Oversight Committee annually for approval. The reason is that Data Governance will be interfacing with other parts of the enterprise, and so it is important to ensure that the strategy succeeds and does not cause any problems. Data Governance units are relatively new in most organizations, so other units are not used to dealing with them. The members of the Data Policy Oversight Committee who are from outside Data Governance can also help to prepare the way to work with some units.

Policy gap analysis is one of the very core capabilities that needs to be established in a Data Governance unit. It significantly improves data management in specific areas of the business, perhaps more than any technology capability like a data catalog. Data Governance units that ignore policy gap analysis will almost certainly be ineffective.

Processing of Policy Requests

Policy requests, from whatever source they come from, are to be considered by the Data Policy Oversight Committee. Normally, this body meets monthly and considers all new policy requests received since the previous meeting as part of the agenda.

Delaying consideration of policy requests, especially from outside Data Governance, would be a significant mistake as it would give the impression that the committee does not care about them. Therefore, consideration of all new policy requests must be a permanent agenda item for all regular meetings.

The committee should have sufficient information about each request to process it. The committee can decide to:

- Accept the policy request and begin to have it processed as a policy action.

- Reject the policy request, with justification.

- Ask for more information about the policy request to arrive at a decision. Hopefully, this will be rare, as the Policy Registrar should have gathered all the required information.

- Defer consideration of the policy request until the next meeting. This should be a rare decision, as it is only really justified if the committee does not have the time or resources for consideration.

- Accept the policy request but put further processing on hold. This is reasonable given that policy work is resource-consumptive and only so much can be done at one time.

The decision must be documented in the minutes of the meeting. For this reason, the Policy Registrar should ideally be the Secretary of the Data Policy Oversight Committee in order to handle the communications seamlessly.

For each policy request considered, the Policy Registrar will update the fields for the committee's decision in the Policy Request Log. The Policy Registrar will also notify the requestor of the decision.

For policy requests that are approved, even if they are on hold, the Policy Registrar will create a new entry in the Policy Portfolio if the request is for a new policy. Otherwise, the Policy Registrar will update the record for an existing policy that will change.

Reporting of Policy Request Processing

If we go back to transparency being one of the most important values for data policy work (and data governance in general), then we should be transparent about how policy requests have been processed.

We can do this in two ways:

- Make the minutes of the Data Policy Oversight Committee available for anyone in the enterprise. The Data Governance unit should have an intranet site where these minutes can be posted directly, or linked to.

- Put a view of the Policy Request Log online to see the status of all policy requests. This view should include every policy request ever added, along with the current status. Of course, such a view will include historical information about policy requests that are no longer active because they have been fulfilled or rejected. This is the point—anyone in the enterprise can see how each policy request has been handled.

Ideally, we adopt both methods.

If there are specific people or business units that must be informed of the status of requests, the best way to achieve this is to add them to the distribution list of the minutes of the Data Policy Oversight Committee. Such additions may be at the discretion of the committee Secretary, or may need a vote by the committee.

Implications for the Policy of Policies

The processing of policy requests highlights the need for certain elements of the policy of policies:

- The obligation of the Data Policy Oversight Committee to consider policy requests for approval.

- The obligation of Data Governance, including the Data Policy Operations Committee, to identify the need for new and updated data policies.

- The right of anyone in the enterprise to make a policy request, and the equal treatment of all policy requests.

- The role and responsibilities of the Policy Registrar.

- The establishment and management of the Policy Request Log.

## Chapter 13

Policy Formulation

P olicy formulation is the creation of a new or updated draft for a data policy, and it is probably the most obvious part of data policy work.

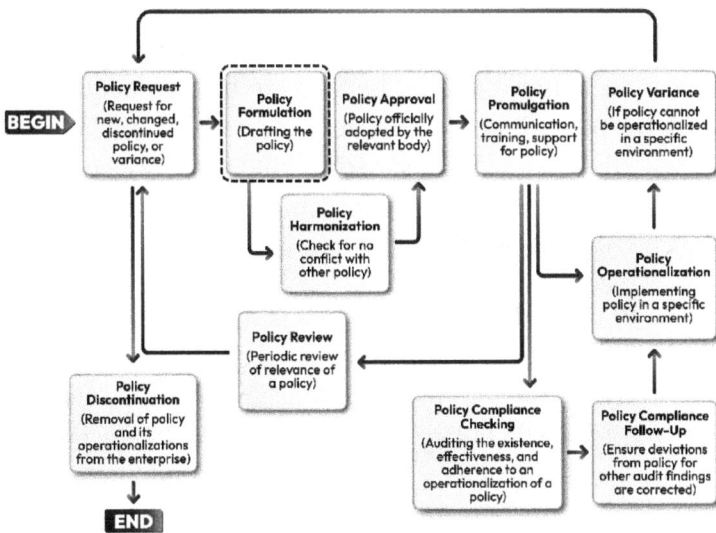

Figure 13.1: Policy Formulation in the Policy Lifecycle

Unfortunately, for some Data Governance units, it is the only part of the policy lifecycle that gets completed, and these units end up with draft policies that never get implemented. Any serious effort at data policy work needs to recognize that policy formulation is one phase in a well-defined policy lifecycle, as we continuously emphasize in this book. But even policy formulation is more than just the writing of the draft policy, as we will now see.

Actioning a Policy Request

For simplicity, we will look at policy formulation for new policies. This obviously means that a policy request has been considered and approved by the Data Policy Oversight Committee or whatever equivalent body has overall accountability for data policies.

It is not simply a matter of the committee approving a request for a new policy. There has to be a procedure that is then engaged to do the policy formulation. We will discuss the procedure shortly, but first, we need to understand that, in general terms, there are three main roles involved in policy formulation:

- **Policy Administrator:** This is someone who makes sure the policy gets developed on time, within scope, and conforms to any standards for policy drafts. The Policy Administrator must be from Data Governance. There is only one per policy.

- **Subject Matter Expert (SME):** Someone who has a sufficient understanding of the policy area so that they can contribute to drafting the policy. There has to be at least one, and there can be several. Depending on the policy, they may or may not be from Data Governance.

- **Stakeholder:** Someone who is not an SME but will be affected by the policy. They cannot contribute to the drafting process, but they can provide feedback on the feasibility of implementation and the level of effort required to implement the data policy. There do not have to be any stakeholders, or there can be one or several.

The Data Policy Oversight Committee must identify the Policy Administrator. The policy request has become a policy action after approval by the committee, and one person must be accountable for shepherding it through to implementation. Data Governance should recommend the Policy Administrator as part of the policy request, and the Policy Administrator should attend the committee meeting where the request is approved to understand any suggestions committee members might have.

Maybe the committee can identify some SMEs, but maybe not. The committee may suggest where to look for SMEs. The Policy Administrator will likely need to go back to Data Governance and ask within the unit for suggestions about SMEs. Data Governance itself may have the expertise and can supply all the needed SMEs. Otherwise, SMEs will need to be recruited from elsewhere. If Data Governance has established a Data Steward network, the Data Stewards can be asked for suggestions. In some cases, external consultants may be required, although this will not work for policies that require a good understanding of how the enterprise works.

Recruiting the SMEs after they have been identified is the next step.

One principle that should be established is that important knowledge about data must be shared and preserved.

The policy of policies can have a statement added to it to reflect this principle, such that if SMEs with relevant knowledge of data are called upon to contribute to policy formulation, they are expected to do so. Once the SMEs have been identified, the Policy Administrator should request their participation using a standard message template. Of course, SMEs should be approached in a diplomatic manner, and their managers should be informed of the request to participate in policy formulation before the SMEs are even contacted. There should also be some kind of incentivization or recognition for SMEs. Perhaps after a policy is promulgated, there can be an informal office party, gift cards can be distributed, or a physical object with the names of the policy team on it can be commissioned.

The stakeholders do not have to be identified immediately, as they will review the policy draft after it is created. Data Governance, the Data Stewards, and the policy formulation team should be able to come up with suggestions for stakeholders. In terms of incentivization, stakeholders will likely want to participate as they will want to know what the policy is about and how they may be affected.

Going back to the Data Policy Oversight Committee meeting where the policy request was approved, the committee can direct the establishment of a working group to formulate the policy. A working group will provide added formality, which is good, given that policies are such powerful tools. Of course, we only need to identify the Policy Administrator at this point, and the decision of the committee will have to recognize that the Policy Administrator will need to form the working group, and may or may not have to confirm to the committee at a later date that it has been formed. A template Terms of Reference can be used for all working groups.

Drafting the Policy

We will assume that a working group has been established to draft a new data policy and it has SMEs from both Data Governance and other organizational units.

The Policy Administrator will need to schedule regular meetings for the working group to draft the policy. Ideally, these should be at least weekly so people do not forget what happened at the previous meeting. The number of meetings required will vary depending on the complexity of the policy, the scope of expertise of the SMEs, and other factors. A maximum of three months should be allocated to formulate a policy.

The process relies on the knowledge of the SMEs. Research can help address knowledge gaps. Unfortunately, today, research means searching the Internet, which can be problematic. Information found online, including from AI, may be of very questionable quality, but the poor quality is not always immediately apparent. It may also lack the details required to draft a policy. If these kinds of problems occur, the working group can report back to the Data Policy Oversight Committee and request additional SME support, which usually means hiring one or more knowledgeable outside consultants.

If a working group gets into these difficulties and cannot find a solution, like outside consultants, then it may have to inform the Data Policy Oversight Committee that it is unable to formulate the policy. The committee will then have to find a solution.

Assuming the working group can proceed, it is extremely difficult to just start writing the policy in a linear manner from the start to the finish in well-polished prose. A better approach is simply for participants to contribute ideas they think should be in the policy. These ideas can be discussed, and the ones the group feels are worthwhile can be retained in a list. The ideas do not have to be particularly well stated at this point or in any particular order.

Once the ideas are captured, they can be grouped into any sets that deal with a specific topic, and sequenced where one idea depends on a preceding one.

At this point, we can draft the policy statements in their final language. We will discuss style and format in later chapters. Once the policy statements are complete, the remaining elements of the policy can be written, such as the scope, audience, etc. Again, we will discuss these in detail later.

The title of the policy should be one of the last things to finalize. It should be clear, as short as possible, and indicate the subject matter of the data policy. Figure 13.2 illustrates this part of policy formulation.

Figure 13.2: High Level Summary of Policy Drafting Process

Stakeholder Review

Once the draft of the new policy is complete, the working group has the option to conduct a stakeholder review. In practice, this seems to be done rarely for data policies, but it is a good idea.

It is important to set expectations with stakeholders for what we require of them, in particular:

- **Understandability:** Can the stakeholders understand the policy based on the draft alone? No additional detailed explanations about the policy should be provided to the stakeholders in order to get reliable feedback on this point.

- **Operationalization Feasibility:** Policies are rather blunt tools in some respects. Governments are sometimes accused of "unfunded mandates" where policies are introduced that cost a lot to comply with, but the government does not provide the funds needed for compliance. We need to detect if operationalization is a serious problem for the new data policy.

- **Stakeholder Role:** Stakeholders need to understand that they are being requested to provide feedback in an advisory role. They do not have a veto on the policy. Optionally, they can be provided with anonymity if they desire it. Stakeholders should also not request feedback from others unless the working group agrees to it. What is needed here are the real thoughts of the stakeholders themselves, not someone else.

Alternatives to Stakeholder Review

There are a couple of other ways to obtain feedback if the process just outlined is impractical for any reason:

- **Data Steward Network:** Data Governance units often establish a network of Data Stewards. What Data Stewards do varies from organization to organization, but in some cases, they are strongly linked to the Data Governance unit. In these situations, the Data Stewards can be requested to provide feedback. For more general policies that affect a broad range of the enterprise, this is probably a good idea. Data Stewards may find it more difficult to provide meaningful feedback on more narrowly focused policies, as they do not have the required domain knowledge.

- **General Consultation:** In this scenario, the draft policy can be put on the Intranet and comments from any interested party can be requested. This is akin to the ways some governmental agencies develop new regulations. The downside risk is that the comments may be from people who have little domain expertise or who ask for further clarifications, which should not be necessary if the draft policy is well written. Of course, if the draft policy really is difficult to understand, such feedback is welcome. An advantage of this approach is that it is the most transparent.

- **No Stakeholder Review:** As mentioned earlier, this is the most common approach. It has the advantage of improving the speed of operationalizing the draft policy since no review period is required. The downside is that operationalization risks may remain undetected.

Processing Stakeholder Feedback

Stakeholders need to be given a finite time to respond, and four weeks seems to be a reasonable timeframe. Reminders may need to be sent to stakeholders who have not responded at the end of weeks two and three.

The working group should process all stakeholder feedback received only after the review period formally ends. This ensures all stakeholders are treated equally.

The working group should analyze the feedback to understand:

- **Draft Clarity:** Determine if the policy draft needs to be amended to make it more understandable. If it does, the draft can be revised and a final draft produced.

- **Implementation Feasibility and Effort:** The feedback from stakeholders can give some idea of the ease or difficulty of implementation. This assessment can be passed back to the Data Policy Oversight Committee. The working group does not have a veto on the policy – that is up to the committee.

At this point, the draft policy can be presented to the Data Policy Oversight Committee for approval.

Committee Approval

After the draft is completed, the Policy Administrator needs to get the approval of the draft policy on the agenda for the next meeting of the Data Policy Oversight Committee. There is a more formal approval phase later on in the policy lifecycle, but the approval at this point is to proceed with next steps. Committee approvals should be prioritized agenda items as the overall policy lifecycle can be quite lengthy.

The working group should not only present the final draft to the committee, but also report on any difficulties and important decisions made during the drafting process as well as any stakeholder feedback received. This will allow the committee to make a meaningful decision to approve the policy draft or not, rather than simply provide an automatic approval.

Ideally, the committee will approve the policy draft. If it does not, then it should place the policy on hold for further consideration. However, approval should be the outcome in almost all cases.

Rejecting the policy outright at this point would give the impression that the efforts of the working group and stakeholders were a waste of time, which would diminish the prestige of the committee and the Data Governance unit. Policies placed on hold can be considered at subsequent meetings by the committee. Maybe the working group can be assigned to redraft it to deal with specific points. Or maybe the policy can be put on a long-term hold until the enterprise is better prepared to operationalize it. Such holds should not be permitted to last for more than a non-renewable period of 12 months following the presentation of the final draft to the committee by the working group, after which the policy effort will be automatically cancelled. These considerations should be included in the policy of policies.

If the committee approves the policy, it can set the time period for the policy to be operationalized. The more difficult the policy is to operationalize, the longer this period can be. What needs to be set is a final date after which everyone in the enterprise must comply.

With the draft policy now approved, the Policy Administrator can update the Policy Portfolio with the information for the formulation phase. Note that the working group is not disbanded at this point, but has to be available in case any issues need to be dealt with in the policy harmonization and policy approval phases. Figure 13.3 summarizes the overall process in policy formulation.

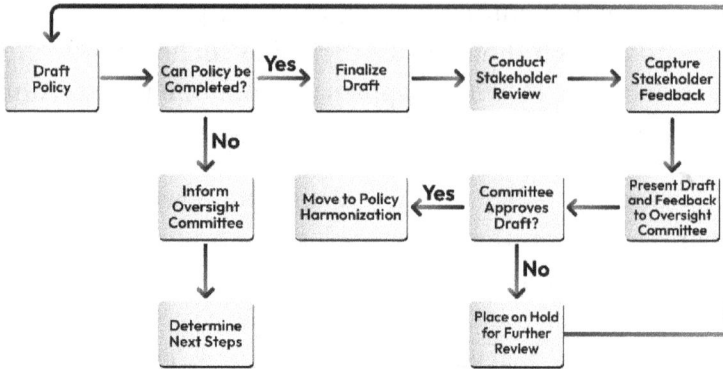

Figure 13.3: High-Level Summary of Policy Formulation Process

Policy Formulation Effort

The processes discussed in this section require a good deal of effort and can take a significant amount of time. Indeed, to some people, they may seem to be too bureaucratic. However, it should be remembered that policies are powerful tools that impact a lot of people in the enterprise and, consequently, should be the best work product possible. Also, policies may remain in force for years, perhaps decades. On this timescale, the policy formulation process, even if it seems lengthy, is very short in comparison.

## Chapter 14

Terminology in Policies

When drafting a policy, it is very important to manage and control the terms being used. There are a number of reasons for this, including:

- Readers need to be able to easily understand the content of the policy.

- Terms have definitions, and the definitions are therefore part of the policy.

- The same terms should have the same meanings in different policies, or readers will be confused.

- A new term should not be created if there is an existing one in order to prevent unnecessary complexity.

However, terminological management is not as easy as it may appear, and special attention needs to be paid to it during the drafting process.

Common and Specialized Terms

"Common Terms" are terms that the average speaker of a language would be expected to know the definition of. "Specialized Terms" are terms used in a particular domain of human experience, like data management, that the average speaker of a language is not expected to be familiar with. In the discipline of Terminology, "Specialized Terms" are normally called "Technical Terms" but a lot of people think that "Technical Terms" are only related to computers and the IT industry, so we will use "Specialized Terms" instead.

An issue with a Specialized Term in a data policy is that readers may not have a clear idea of its definition.

Perhaps they have heard the term before, and perhaps they have some idea of what it means, but that is insufficient to be able to read and understand a policy. The situation is even more problematic for readers who have never heard of a term used in a data policy.

Terminology issues can also arise when a Common Term is used as a Specialized Term in a policy, and has a completely different definition from the Common Term. For example:

- "Retention" in common parlance means keeping things.

- "Retention" in data management means processes for getting rid of data that must not or should not be kept for longer.

The best way to avoid terminology problems is to:

- Ensure the most widely used Specialized Terms are adopted when there is a choice of several Specialized Terms for the same concept.

- Make Specialized Terms stand out in the policy text.

- Provide definitions for all Specialized Terms.

Centralized Business Glossary

Given this last requirement, some kind of centralized control of terms is required, and the best way to do that today is to implement a centralized Business Glossary. This is yet another metadata requirement for policy work.

A Business Glossary is a computerized tool for managing terms and their definitions. It is nearly always web-based, and is usually a component of a larger tool known as a Data Catalog that provides support for the overall data governance and data management needs of an enterprise.

Although this sounds complicated, a Business Glossary is, at heart, a simple list and any enterprise should be able to develop one quickly. A major requirement, however, is for staff in the enterprise to be able to work collaboratively in the Business Glossary. This means that standalone files like spreadsheets are less suitable. Simple SaaS (Cloud-hosted Software-as-a-Service) tools that emulate spreadsheets and relational databases are much better candidates. Of course, if an enterprise has a Data Catalog, it will have a Business Glossary and should be used.

A great deal has been and could be written about Business Glossaries, but what might a Business Glossary look like just to be able to deal with policies, ignoring other use cases? Table 14.1 is a set of columns that could be included in a simple Business Term table in a Business Glossary for policy needs. Of course, there are many other requirements that might influence the design of a Business Glossary, but Table 14.1 is a reasonable list of policy work.

The design in Table 14.1 emphasizes the role of a Preferred Term. A Preferred Term is the term to use when there are several synonyms for the same concept. It is important to use Preferred Terms in policies wherever possible, rather than any synonym, to make understanding easier for the reader. Sometimes this is not possible because terms come from laws and regulations for a particular policy, and in the context of that policy, they are the Preferred Terms.

Column	Description	Applies to Record	Datatype	Mandatory?
Term	Any Specialized Term used in the business. Common Terms (those used in everyday English whose meaning is widely understood) are also included if they have some special meaning in the business.	Every record has a value.	Short Text	Yes

Column	Description	Applies to Record	Datatype	Mandatory?
Context	The context of the Business term. Often a term is enterprise-wide, and in such cases, this item can be blank. But a particular definition may exist for a specific policy. So, the same terms can have different definitions in different policies. The policy name is the Context if this is the case. Note that in such cases, the term alone cannot be used for uniqueness in the table because there will be duplicates. Some kind of identifier column will need to be added to provide uniqueness (not shown here).	Only record for a Preferred Term has a value.	Short Text	Conditional. Must state the context if the scope of the term is less than enterprise-wide.
Short Definition	The official definition of the business term. For a policy, this is exactly what is intended for the policy.	Only record for a Preferred Term has a value.	Long Text	Mandatory

Column	Description	Applies to Record	Datatype	Mandatory?
Long Definition	If needed, this is more of an explanation of the Business Term. This may go beyond a definition to include, for example, how to use the Business Term. This should NOT be used for terms that appear in policies, as it can confuse the reader. Only the Short Definition is permitted for these terms. However, it may sometimes be useful for terms not used in policies.	Only record for a Preferred Term has a value.	Long Text	Conditional, but not to be used for policy terms.
Is Preferred Term	Where there are several synonyms for the same concept, this is the term that should be used in the enterprise.	Every record has a value.	Y/N	Mandatory
Is Expanded Term	For an Abbreviation (including Acronyms), this is the Business Term that is fully expanded based on the Abbreviation. It may or may not be a Preferred Term.	Every record has a value.	Y/N	Mandatory

Column	Description	Applies to Record	Datatype	Mandatory?
Source Type	The type of source that the definition came from. This may be important for policies if the term and definition came from a regulation. Must be one of: Document, Subject Matter Expert, Database, Metadata Store.	Only record for a Preferred Term has a value.	Short Text	Mandatory
Source Name	The name of the source from which the definition came.	Only record for a Preferred Term has a value.	Short Text	Mandatory
Semantic Type	How, if at all, the Business Term is used. Must be one of: Pure Business Concept, Entity Type, Data Element, Instance of something, Reference Data Entry.	Only record for a Preferred Term has a value.	Short Text	Mandatory
Calculation	The description of any logic needed to derive values of the Business Term. Keep such information in this field, rather than the Short or Long Definitions.	Only record for a Preferred Term has a value.	Long Text	Conditional: Needed if this Business Term is a Data Element that is calculated or otherwise derived.

Column	Description	Applies to Record	Datatype	Mandatory?
Is Synonym of	If the Business Term is a synonym of a Preferred Term, such as an acronym, then the Preferred Term is populated in this field. In this way, the record is related to the Preferred Term.	Only for synonyms.	Short Text	Conditional. Only needed if the term is a synonym.
Example	Any examples of how the Business Term is used. Multiple examples are simply concatenated within this field.	Only record for a Preferred Term has a value.	Long Text	Optional
Note	Any additional information that should be captured for the Business Term.	All Terms	Long Text	Optional

Table 14.1: Design of a Business Term Table in a Business Glossary

One additional requirement is that we need to know what Business Terms are used in what policies. This means having a table of policies that is linked to the Business Term table in the Business Glossary. We have already discussed the Policy Portfolio in the preceding chapters. Technically, all we need to do is to implement the Policy Portfolio in the same environment as the Business Glossary and establish a relationship between the two tables. This should be relatively easy.

Adding Policy Terms to a Centralized Business Glossary

An important requirement during policy formulation is for staff drafting a data policy to be able to easily find all the Specialized Terms that have been used in previous data policies. Staff can review this list and reuse the Specialized Terms they need, which will greatly reduce the chances of a new Specialized Term being created that means the same as an existing one.

For this to happen, staff drafting data policies must ensure they populate the Business Glossary with the terms in the draft policy, and relate these terms to the policy. This is probably best done at the point of policy approval, since there are then no doubts about what Business Terms are in the policy. Of course, this is a bit of a risk as the elapsed time from the start of policy formulation to policy approval may be months, and staff drafting other policies may be unaware of how Business Terms are being used in the policies being formulated. Therefore, Data Governance may wish to update the Business Glossary with all Business Terms in all policy drafts, with the understanding that some may not make it through to the final draft that gets approved. These Business Terms will then have to be removed from the Business Glossary.

Access and Security for Policy Business Terms

Business Glossaries are not often thought of as being secure environments. In most enterprises, collaboration is encouraged and people can submit updates to definitions via governed workflows or in some cases, users can directly edit definitions.

This is a potential risk for data policy Business Terms because the definitions are actually part of the policy, although they are managed in the Business Glossary. Therefore, if a definition changes, it is equivalent to issuing a new version of the policy.

New versions of the policy can only be issued as a result of an action by the Data Policy Oversight Committee following the established policy lifecycle. We cannot have *ad hoc* changes happening to the definitions of policy Business Terms housed in the Business Glossary.

The solution is to permit read-only access to policy terms in the Business Glossary and to restrict any form of editing to a policy gatekeeper, the Policy Administrator, for each policy. Furthermore, only the Policy Administrators should be allowed to edit the relationships between Business Terms and data policies. Figure 14.1 illustrates the overall architecture.

A control report of what Business Terms are used in policies and what links between Business Terms and policies have been updated in the past month should be produced at the start of a new month and circulated to all members of the Data Policy Operations Committee. This will prevent unauthorized updates to the Business Terms used in policies.

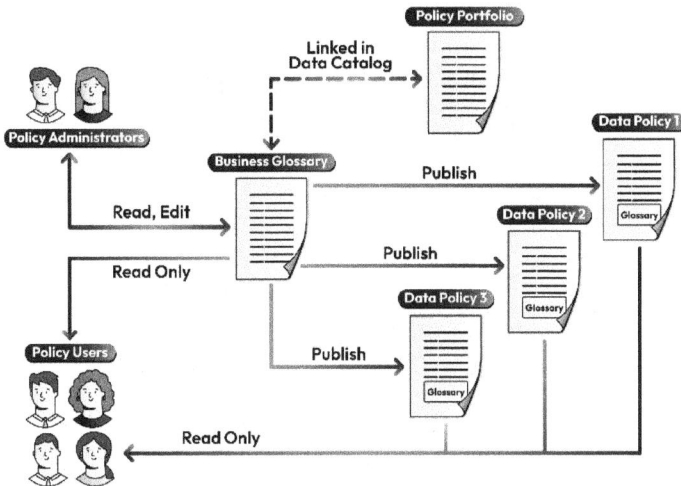

Figure 14.1: High Level View of Architecture for Business Glossary and Data Policies

The access restrictions suggested here can be mandated in the policy of policies. Since many policies are responses to regulation, a lack of such access controls makes the policies vulnerable to unintended changes via unauthorized updates to definitions, which may mean the enterprise is in violation of the regulations. Compliance with regulations is, therefore, yet another reason for these access restrictions.

Interpretation of Business Terms

While access restrictions to control changing the definitions of Business Terms and linkages to data policies is important, there is a need to go even further.

Because of the desire for collaboration in Business Glossaries, they often have features to allow any user to add comments.

What needs to be avoided with Business Terms used in policies is any interpretation of the definitions of these terms, other than that supplied by the staff drafting the policy.

It is easy to envision a circumstance where someone adds some comments about what they think a policy-related Business Term "really" means, and then another person views this in the Business Glossary and assumes these comments are officially approved, because the Business Glossary is a "production" environment.

Therefore, it is highly recommended that all editing features of the Business Glossary be disabled for anyone except Policy Administrators for all policy-related Business Terms.

Author Once, Publish Anywhere

The main reason for using a Business Glossary to manage policy-related Business Terms is to centralize all of them in one place so it is easy to understand and manage the total set that exists and which data policies they are used in. This is in contrast to each data policy having a glossary of terms embedded in it, and managed only in the policy document, which means no single view is possible.

There is also another reason that makes using a Business Glossary valuable. This is the principle of "author once, publish anywhere," which means there should be only one environment in which all policy-related Business Terms are edited. From this environment, the terms and definitions can be published anywhere, including policy documents. However, terms and definitions cannot be edited in any of the environments in which they are published—only in the authoring environment. In our example, we have used a Business Glossary in a data catalog as the tool for authoring. However, many content management platforms support "author once, publish anywhere," and perhaps one of these might be better suited to the needs of some enterprises.

## Chapter 15

Policy Format

We have discussed policy formulation as a process. However, what should the work product of this process, the actual policy, look like?

We can begin by reviewing some problems that we need to avoid.

Problems with Policy Format

A major issue with many policies is that they are formatted as large blocks of text without any consistent format between similar policies in the same organization.

In addition, there is often poor sectioning with, at best, some general titles. Figure 15.1 provides an example.

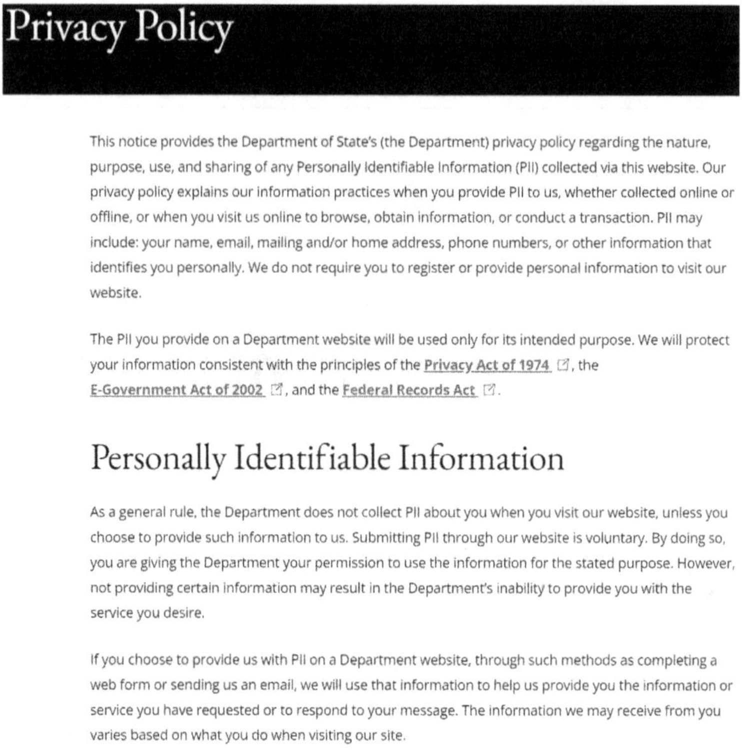

Privacy Policy

This notice provides the Department of State's (the Department) privacy policy regarding the nature, purpose, use, and sharing of any Personally Identifiable Information (PII) collected via this website. Our privacy policy explains our information practices when you provide PII to us, whether collected online or offline, or when you visit us online to browse, obtain information, or conduct a transaction. PII may include: your name, email, mailing and/or home address, phone numbers, or other information that identifies you personally. We do not require you to register or provide personal information to visit our website.

The PII you provide on a Department website will be used only for its intended purpose. We will protect your information consistent with the principles of the **Privacy Act of 1974** ⧉, the **E-Government Act of 2002** ⧉, and the **Federal Records Act** ⧉.

Personally Identifiable Information

As a general rule, the Department does not collect PII about you when you visit our website, unless you choose to provide such information to us. Submitting PII through our website is voluntary. By doing so, you are giving the Department your permission to use the information for the stated purpose. However, not providing certain information may result in the Department's inability to provide you with the service you desire.

If you choose to provide us with PII on a Department website, through such methods as completing a web form or sending us an email, we will use that information to help us provide you the information or service you have requested or to respond to your message. The information we may receive from you varies based on what you do when visiting our site.

Figure 15.1: US State Department Website Privacy Policy

(https://www.state.gov/privacy-policy/ Accessed 2024-07-29)

If a reader has any doubt about a specific point, they may have to read the entire policy from start to finish to try to find any references to what they are looking for.

Of course, it is possible to search for terms, but can the reader be sure they know the correct terms before they try to search? This difficulty is made even worse if the point the reader is looking for is addressed by several parts of the text scattered throughout the policy. The reader has to find these and stitch them together in their mind to try to synthesize what the policy has to say on the point in question.

Not having a consistent format means that the look and feel of each policy are different. This adds to the difficulty of the reader in processing a policy. The reader does not know in advance the schema of a policy and what can be found where in it.

> *We must always remember that staff usually look only occasionally at policies, and when they do, they typically need a quick answer to a specific point. Staff do not want to spend time decoding the structure of the policy to figure out where to look in it.*

Let's consider an example of how to format a data policy.

Policy Header

When viewing a policy, the reader needs to know immediately what policy it is. This is best expressed in a distinct header section. An example appears in Figure 15.2.

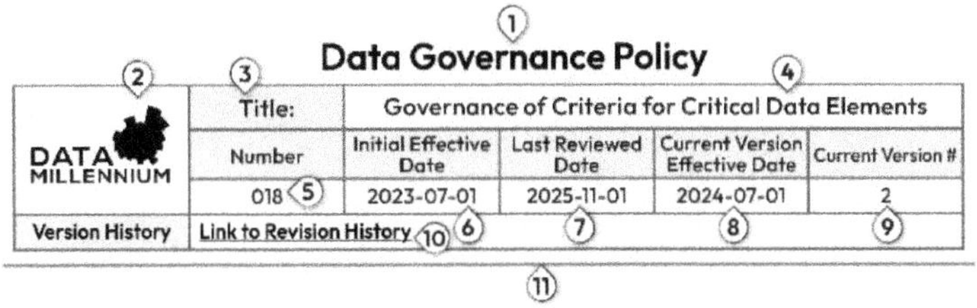

Figure 15.2: *Policy Header*

We will now consider each numbered element shown in the policy header in Figure 5.2 in turn.

1. **Policy Category.** Staff should recognize that a policy is a data policy immediately, and not a policy from Human Resources, Finance, or another unit. The best way to do this is for all data policies to have the same general header. In Figure 15.2, it is "Data Governance Policy," but it could be "Data Policy," "Data Management Policy," or something similar. However, it must be consistent across all data policies. The policy category should be instantly recognizable. In our example, it is placed at the top and is in a large font, perhaps with a different color. Whatever approach is taken, the need for instant recognition must be achieved.

2. **Logo.** Branding is important as it carries a reputational message. Including a logo is a good way to achieve branding, as is done in Figure 15.2. Perhaps the logo is of the enterprise, implying that the policy has enterprise-level endorsement. Perhaps it is a logo of the Data Governance unit, informing the reader of the organizational origin of the policy. Branding provides some form of reassurance to the reader and should be included.

3. **Information Element Names.** The design shown in Figure 15.2 is a block incorporating several information elements. That is, specific information about the policy (shown with a gray background in our example). The information element names should be displayed next to the values of the information elements. If context can easily be

inferred, then a shortened name can be provided, such as "Title" instead of "Policy Title."

Exactly what information elements should be displayed must be decided on before any data policies are formulated, with the possible exception of the policy of policies because this has to be in place before any other data policy can be formulated. The set of information elements shown here is probably the minimum that is required.

4. **Policy Title.** The policy's title must reflect the policy's content as closely as possible. It must also be unique and clearly distinguishable from the title of any other policy (not just data policies). Further, it should indicate the policy is a data policy as staff will have many policies to deal with, the majority of which have nothing to do with data. The title should be as short as possible. Remember that the title will appear not only in the policy document but also in lists of policies, so it must not be confusing.

5. **Policy Number.** A policy may have a policy number in addition to a policy title. In some organizations, a policy number may be mandatory, but in other organizations, it may be optional. In the latter case, it is up to the Data Governance unit to determine if it will use a numbering scheme. This should be decided before any data policies are formulated, although the policy of policies may be excepted. The format of the numbering scheme can be simple, such as an incremented sequence number, or it can be complex, reflecting any

groupings of policies. Once a decision is made, it needs to be stuck to for all data policies going forward.

6. **Initial Effective Date.** This is the date on which the policy enters into force. That is, the date from which it must be complied with and on which the policy begins to be enforced (although occasionally these may be two separate dates). Staff need to be aware of this date. It is confusing to put the date of publication or approval of the policy in the header. These have no relevance to staff, who want to know when they need to comply. This is not to say that these other dates are unimportant, it is just that they do not serve any purpose here.

7. **Last Reviewed Date.** Oddly, this is one of the most important but one of the most overlooked information elements in policies. It is the date on which the policy was last officially reviewed. This review may or may not have resulted in changes to the policy, but the Last Reviewed Date must be updated as a result of all reviews. The importance of this date stems from a general lack of trust in documentation about technology and data that exists generally in every enterprise. Staff often suspect that such documentation is not kept up to date and cannot be trusted. In general, staff begin to distrust documentation that is over a year old, and are highly distrustful of any documentation that is over two years old. This appears to include attitudes to policies, and some staff may feel that a policy does not apply if it is older than two years.

Additionally, staff need some reassurance that the policy is being adjusted to business and technical reality in an active manner, and that the staff is not being put in an impossible position where the business demands one thing and the policy requires another. Having a Last Reviewed Date that clearly indicates the policy is never allowed to go more than one year without being reviewed and possibly updated provides needed reassurance to staff.

8. **Current Version Effective Date.** This information element refers to when the current version comes into force. If the initial version is in force, and there have been no subsequent versions, then this information element should have the same value as the Initial Effective Date. Otherwise, it will be the date on which the current version (the latest version) of the policy must be complied with.

9. **Current Version #.** This is the version number of the current version of the policy. Each enterprise must decide on the version numbering scheme of its data policies. The simplest is probably the best, with versions starting at 1 and being incremented by 1 for each subsequent version. Policies should not change frequently, so a more complex version numbering scheme with, say, "point" versions (version numbers that include digits to the right of the decimal point like "2.09") is not warranted and may cause confusion. Readers must be aware of any new version of the policy that is currently in force and the Current Version # provides it.

10. **Version History.** If the current version of the data policy is anything other than the first version, then staff who have worked with previous versions of the policy need to understand what has changed. A link to a Policy Bulletin (see chapter on policy promulgation) that explains the changes must be included here.

11. **End of Block.** A dividing line indicates the end of the header block. This helps the reader understand the scope of the header.

What Is Not in the Policy Header

The policy header must be as short as possible, as readers do not want to scroll down a long way to get to the policy details. Data Governance staff should, therefore, refrain from putting a lot of administrative detail in the policy header, like who the author was, who approved it, the entire text of the version history, and so on. A reader does not need to know this as a priority, and it can best be placed elsewhere.

Policy Prologue

The next section of a policy should be a prologue, which provides an overview of the policy so that the reader can quickly determine what situations it applies to. Figure 15.3 provides an example.

① Description
This policy identifies governance needs for the development of criteria for identifying Critical Data Elements (CDE's).

② Rationale
CDE's are identified by business units from among the total set of data elements these business units manage. It is important that CDE's are identified in a uniform way across the enterprise.
If data elements that should be CDE's are overlooked, this presents a risk. If data elements that are not CDE's are identified as CDE's, then this will add an unnecessary burden since CDE's require additional governance and management tasks. Therefore, a uniform set of criteria for identifying CDE's must be developed and applied across the enterprise. This policy provides the framework for the governance of these criteria.

③ Scope
All data within the enterprise has the potential to contain CDE's. Therefore, criteria for identifying CDE's apply to all enterprise data, and thus this policy applies to all enterprise data.

④ Audience
All areas of the enterprise involved in any aspect of managing CDE's must comply with this policy.

⑤ _____

Figure 15.3: Policy Prologue Example

The information elements in the policy prologue are:

1. **Description.** A brief summary of what the content of the policy is. The reader can understand the subject matter of the policy clearly in a very short time.

2. **Rationale.** Why the policy is needed. This should be about the objectives of the policy and what it is intended to achieve, rather than a history of how it came to be. Readers are interested in the justifications for policies, as they may feel that some policies are unnecessary burdens. The better a rationale can be explained for a data policy, the better the chances of compliance.

3. **Scope.** It is necessary to say what data, or what data management processes, are covered by the policy and what is not covered by the policy. Very often, all data will be within the scope of a data

policy, but this should be stated explicitly so the reader is not in doubt.

4. **Audience.** Sometimes, this is termed "Who Must Comply." It is the people in the enterprise who have to comply with the policy. Many data policies apply to everyone, but some enterprises have operations in different countries, and a particular policy may only apply to one or a few of these countries. Other enterprises are conglomerates of different operating companies, and a given policy may only apply to one or some of these companies. It is very important to be clear about who has to comply. For consistency, this information element may consist of a set of options that can be appropriately checked for each policy.

5. **End of Prologue.** Again, we use a dividing line to indicate the end of the policy prologue.

Policy Statements

We have finally got to the core of all policy work which is the policy statements. As mentioned earlier, the format of a large "blob" of text should be avoided. Instead, atomic, complete policy statements should be adopted, as shown in Figure 15.4.

①
Policy Statements

② #	Statement ④	Explanation ⑥
③ 1	The Data Governance Unit develops the criteria for determining if a data element is a CDE or not. ⑤ This list of criteria can be accessed by any enterprise staff.	Enterprise staff are provided with a standardized set of criteria to enable them to determine if a data element is a CDE or not. This provides transparency and uniformity across the enterprise.enterprise staff.
2	The Data Governance Unit will develop a process for managing the list of CDE identification criteria that is consultative.	In this way, business units can influence the criteria. While the Data Governance Unit can propose some criteria centrally, it is important to get feedback from the business on (a) what criteria the business may feel are important; and (b) whether proposed criteria can be used without undue effort.

Figure 15.4: Policy Statements

We will now review the information elements here.

1. **Section Title.** This clearly states that we are in the policy statements section. The policy statements are what must be complied with.

2. **Table Header.** The policy statements are expressed as rows in a table, each with a number, a statement, and an explanation of the statement. The table header names each column.

3. **Policy Statement Number.** Each policy statement has a number. There is not really any other way to identify a policy statement and refer to it easily. The numbering format can vary. It may be a straight sequence number such as 1, 2, 3, 4,..., or we may group policy statements together into sections with a "point" format such as 1.1, 1.2, 2.1, 2.2, 2.3,... The numbering of policy statements is another huge advantage over the "blob" of text approach.

4. **Policy Statement.** A policy statement must be atomic, meaning it only deals with one thing. It must be self-contained, meaning that it deals with

something completely. Thus, the reader does not need to search elsewhere within the policy to find other policy statements necessary to fully understand the point being made. The statement does not have to be only a single sentence, but it should not become a large block of text either.

5. **Policy Sub-statement.** Sometimes, but not always, having some additional information about the policy statement is valuable. This can be put underneath the policy statement as is done here. The policy statement can be in bold to distinguish it from the policy sub-statement. This feature should be used only when absolutely necessary, and it is best avoided if possible.

6. **Explanation.** An explanation is a way of bringing a mind to an understanding of something. A policy statement is a reference that must be precise. An explanation can elaborate some of the policy statement's concepts, give examples, or provide a rationale. However, it must not itself be a policy statement.

Glossary

We have already discussed the need for management of Specialized Terms in the chapter on terminology. In that chapter, we took the approach that Specialized Terms are best managed in the Business Glossary. However, each policy should contain a glossary of its Specialized Terms. This conforms to the principle of "locality of reference," which holds that all required information should be available in one place.

By having a glossary of terms in a policy, the reader can immediately review the definition of a Specialized Term without having to link to a Business Glossary to which they may not even have access rights.

A technical solution needs to be found to implement the "author once, publish anywhere" principle in this situation. That is, the Business Glossary may contain the managed set of Specialized Terms for the policy in question, and it must be possible to create an output from the Business Glossary that is the glossary of terms needed for the particular data policy involved. Perhaps some formatting work will still need to be done, but nothing more should be needed.

Figure 15.5 provides an example of a glossary section in a policy.

Glossary ②

①

See also the Consolidated Data Governance Glossary for terms and definitions used in all policies.

③

Term	Definition
CDE ④	See "Critical Data Element" ⑤
Critical Data Element	An especially important data element that requires more governance and management than regular data elements.
Metadata	Information used to understand and manage the data assets of the enterprise.

Figure 15.5: Policy Glossary

The information elements in the glossary are:

1. **Section Title.** This clearly states we are in a glossary section.

2. **Data Catalog Reference.** This is needed if Specialized Terms in all policies are also curated in the enterprise data catalog's Business Glossary. A link in the text here will lead to the Business Glossary. The data catalog was covered in the chapter on terminology.

3. **Table Header.** It is best to keep the glossary as simple as possible, and a table format works well. For further simplicity, only the Term and Definition are shown. The reader should not need to see anything more than these two items.

4. **Term.** This is a Specialized Term that occurs in the policy. Do not include terms not found in the policy.

5. **Definition.** This is the curated enterprise definition for the term **as it applies to the policy**. It is extremely important to understand this point. The meaning of a particular term may be different in contexts other than the policy.

   If the term is an acronym, then it must simply point to the fully expanded term, which is another entry in the glossary that will have the definition.

Related Documents

There may optionally be a section for related documents. These are documents that are closely related to the policy, and it may benefit the reader to know about them. However, the documents must have a close connection to the policy, otherwise readers may be confused. Figure 15.6 shows an example.

Related Documents

Type	Name/ Number/ Link	Relationship to Policy
Policy	Identification of Critical Data Elements	How to apply this policy
Policy	Information to be Maintained for Critical Data Elements	What information to collect when applying this policy
Checklist	Critical Data Element Identification Checklist	The criteria generated from this policy
Glossary	Consolidated Data Governance Glossary	Definitions of specialized terms used in this policy

Figure 15.6: Related Documents Section

The information elements here are as follows:

1. **Section Title.** This clearly shows the section is for related documents.
2. **Table Header.** It is best to keep the information in the table to the minimum the reader has to know. There should not be any detailed description of the documents.
3. **Type.** This indicates if the related document is a policy or another type of document. Obviously, policies are more important documents, so it is helpful to inform the reader of which documents are policies.
4. **Name / Number / Link.** Whatever official title or identity the document has should come next. It could be a name or a number. It should not be a description, but the official identity. Having this as a link to the actual document can be helpful.

However, there is always the danger of a link being broken because the document is moved somewhere else, changes in some way, or is deleted. This can be fixed during the annual review of the policy, so it is a risk that Data Governance should weigh carefully.

5. **Relationship to Policy.** This describes how the document is related to the policy.

Support

The policy should conclude with details of how to obtain support. Providing an email address is the most common option, but it should not be for a specific person. Rather, it should be a general email address for Data Governance. Figure 15.7 provides an example.

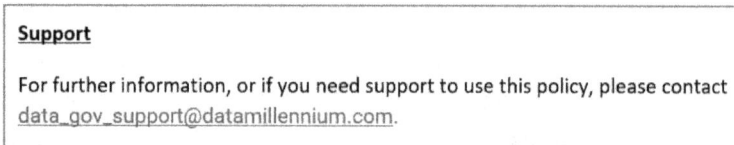

> **Support**
>
> For further information, or if you need support to use this policy, please contact data_gov_support@datamillennium.com.

Figure 15.7: Policy Support Details

Confidentiality and Security Markings

Most enterprises require that their policies have a security classification of at least Business Confidential, which usually means that the enterprise does not permit policies to be distributed or accessed externally. The Data Governance unit must determine what confidentiality and security markings need to be put on policies. Figure 15.8 provides a simple example where the markings are put in the footer area of a document.

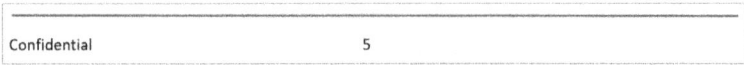

Confidential	5

Figure 15.8: Simple Confidentiality Marking

Some policies may have higher security and confidentiality levels than others. This is something that should be determined during the drafting process.

Other Format Elements

Sometimes, there is a desire to add change history to a policy because change history is frequently included in other types of documents. However, this is unnecessary, given that a link to the version history is provided in the header block. It does not supply any additional information the reader may need and may conflict with the official version history.

Add the author's name if this information is useful. Names of approvers and dates of approval can also be added if needed. As noted before, policy administration information is of questionable use to the average reader and is best stored elsewhere, such as in the metadata being curated for all policies.

Of course, enterprises may have additional specific format elements that they wish to add beyond those discussed here. This is fine as long as the schema of the policy is decided initially and changed rarely if at all. Readers greatly appreciate consistency in documents, especially documents they may only read infrequently. We need to make it as easy as possible for readers to consume policies.

Definitions of Information Elements

We have reviewed quite a lot of information elements in this chapter, such as "Last Reviewed Date." What these information elements mean may seem obvious to Data Governance, which manages policies, but the meaning may be less clear to other staff, especially new joiners. Therefore, Data Governance should consider adding information elements with definitions to the Business Glossary, where they can be managed centrally. These terms and their definitions can also be added to the glossary of terms in the actual policy document. Readers can then easily understand what they mean.

Implications for Policy of Policies

Most of what we have discussed in this chapter is standards for data policies. These standards will have to be developed by Data Governance. How to develop and manage standards is a quite different topic to policies, and we cannot cover it in this book. What can be done, however, is to include a statement in the policy of policies that Data Governance will develop all necessary standards for data policies. There should be no mention of the content of these standards as that would be far too detailed for any policy of policies.

## Chapter 16

Data Policy Style

We have discussed the format of a policy, but what about the textual content? How should we write the text during policy formulation? To answer these questions, we must think about the principles related to what we want to accomplish with data policies. Important principles should include:

- **Consistency.** The textual component of data policies cannot vary wildly from policy to policy in terms of its style. This will reduce readability.

  Principle: Data policy style must be as uniform as possible across all data policies.

- **Recognizability.** Specialized Terms should be clearly distinguishable from Common Terms so the reader can be alerted that they may need to consult a definition.

  Principle: Specialized Terms must be immediately recognizable as such.

- **Clarity.** The policy text must tell the reader what to do in an understandable way.

  Principle: The text of a data policy must need as little interpretation as possible.

- **Brevity.** People are overwhelmed with information. Data policies should not add to this.

  Principle: A data policy must convey its meaning clearly with as few words as possible.

Different enterprises may have specific needs that require other principles, but it is important for a Data Governance unit to think carefully about what it is trying to achieve with the reader of a data policy and formulate principles for policy style accordingly.

Policy Style Guide

There are a lot of possible elements that can guide how policies are written, so it is a good idea to incorporate them into a Policy Style Guide.

Since data policies are usually written intermittently, there is no guarantee that anyone can remember the style rules without such an aid.

It may also be difficult to infer all of the rules by looking at older policies that supposedly have the correct style, especially for new joiners in a Data Governance unit.

The Data Policy Operations Committee should develop a Policy Style Guide. If necessary, external consultants can be used to help, but the guide must be aligned with the culture and operating environment of the enterprise.

Once the guide is written, the Data Policy Operations Committee should have it approved by the Data Policy Oversight Committee since this committee oversees the entire policy lifecycle.

The policy of policies will have been written by this time, but it should mandate the development of a Policy Style Guide to be approved by the Data Policy Oversight Committee, after which it will be a standard for the writing of data policies. In this way, the Policy Style Guide will become an official part of the policy lifecycle that cannot be ignored.

If the Policy Style Guide is not officially adopted in this way, then staff will eventually just forget about it and write data policies in an *ad hoc* manner. Furthermore, there will be no institutional continuity due to personnel changes in Data Governance, especially in leadership. A Policy Style Guide that is not officially adopted may be seen as "old" by new leadership, who will may see no reason to follow it.

Style Resources

There may be various resources, or even standards, for style that already exist within the enterprise before work even starts on data policies. Technical writing standards are one example. These should be consulted for anything that can be used in writing policies.

Public resources are available, too. An example is RuleSpeak (https://www.rulespeak.com/en/). This is a set of guidelines for expressing business rules. While rules are not policies, they are somewhat close. RuleSpeak offers useful advice that we can adopt.

If there is a style guide for policies in general in the enterprise, then this will have to be followed. It is unlikely that data policies will be so different from other enterprise policies that something different would be required. However, if no such general guide exists, one will need to be created.

Style Checklist

While every enterprise will be different, it is possible to think of some general guidelines for writing a Policy Style Guide for data policies. Some suggestions appear in Table 16.1.

#	Guideline
1	**Terminology**
1.1	If acronyms are used, the first occurrence must be in parentheses following the fully expanded term. Example: "European Union (EU)."
1.2	When a Specialized Term is used, it must be capitalized to distinguish it from other words in the context in which it appears. Example: "A formal procedure must be established for Data Issue Management so that resolutions can be efficiently arrived at." Here, "Data Issue Management" is a Specialized Term.

#	Guideline
1.3	A Specialized Term must be hyperlinked to its definition where it first occurs in each section of the policy. This will aid readers who focus on a particular section. The definition will be in the Glossary section of the policy.
1.4	All Specialized Terms must have their definitions validated. Example: "Third Normal Form" is a Specialized Term, and Data Architecture should provide its definition. Make sure the policy uses these terms correctly. If not, the policy can be confusing.

2	**Imperative Form**
2.1	The active voice, rather than the passive voice, must be used wherever possible. Example: "The SME writes the policy" must be used instead of: "The policy is written by the SME."
2.2	Use the word "must" to emphasize that there is only one way to conform to the policy statement. Do not use "can," "shall," "should" as they suggest the policy statement may be optional. Do not use "must not"; rather use the style of universal negation in point 3.2 below.
2.3	Only use "may" and "may not" to indicate that something is optional, and always state the conditions under which it is optional.
2.4	Do not use "would" or "could." These words will make it impossible for a reader to understand whether a policy statement is mandatory or optional.

3	**Quantification**
3.1	A policy statement that applies universally to a range of instances must use the word "all" rather than something else, like "each" or "every." Example: "All data issues must be recorded in a database."
3.2	A policy statement that universally prohibits something across a range of instances must use "no" rather than something else, like "none" or "never." Example: "No Data Quality Issue Resolution must cause a further problem."

#	Guideline

3.3	Sometimes, a policy statement must enumerate a list of instances it applies to. Also, if a policy statement has exceptions, then these should be clearly itemized in a bulleted list. Example: "A minimum set of standard data elements and values must be recorded for every data issue:
	   • Unique Identifier
	   • Issue Classification
	   • Issue Description
	   • Submitter Details."

3.4	Avoid using modifiers that cannot be measured or have not been defined. Instead, always explain why you are using the term. Example:
	   • "Key" component – instead, say, "The application will not run without it, because …"
	   • "Sufficient" (or "adequate") resources – instead, say, "Resources must be sufficient to attain…" [what identifiable or measurable state?]
	   • "User friendly" interface – instead, explain what makes it "friendly" to a user.
	Other examples:
	   • "Critical" process
	   • "Essential" detail
	   • "Significant" modification

3.5	When using terms such as "minimize" or "maximize," always reference a measurable standard. Example: "Reduce the level of risk to a minimum [what value?] by [performing what action?] …"
4	**General Guidance**
4.1	Only use "you" or "yours" when any other way of writing the policy statement makes it more difficult to read.
4.2	Always use a shorter word instead of a longer word if possible.
4.3	Always use a more frequently used word instead of a less frequently used one.

#	Guideline
4.4	Only use words that are needed. If it is possible to remove a word without losing meaning, then do so. Always ask yourself why each word is needed and what confusion it avoids. If you cannot find a good reason, then remove the word.
4.5	Use strong rather than weak words, even if the latter are considered more refined. English words with Germanic roots are nearly always stronger than English words with Latin roots, even though their meanings may be identical, such as "hearty welcome" vs. "cordial reception."
4.6	Do not use "support" except to describe true support functions such as a Help Desk.
4.7	Be careful about using nouns that are also used as verbs. Make sure the meaning is clear every time one is used. Example: "Record" is used to mean a unit of storage composed of a set of data elements. But "record" is also used to mean the act of recording something. That is, capturing something about it as data. So, it is possible to say, "The system used this record to record the customer details." Such a sentence is difficult to understand. Similarly, "interface" is used both as a noun and a verb, such as for things and actions.
4.8	Ensure each policy statement is atomic. It should cover one and only one idea that is to be operationalized by a reader. Example: "Risk aggregation must ensure data quality is checked, data lineage is documented, and manual checks are carried out." This statement has three different ideas in it, each of which would need to be implemented in a very different way. It should be split up into three different policy statements.

5	References
5.1	Do not include a policy statement from another policy. Instead, reference the statement in the other policy. If a policy statement is copied into many policies and then has to be changed, it will be difficult to find all the places where it has to be changed.

#	Guideline
5.2	Wherever possible, do not refer to individual people but instead to roles or functions.
	People leave positions. If this happens, updating the policy and issuing a new version will be necessary. Minimize this kind of change.
5.3	Wherever possible, do not include individual locations, names of organizational units, individual email addresses, or individual telephone numbers.
	These items are subject to change. Refer to group email addresses and general telephone numbers. Refer to roles or functions rather than locations and organizational units.
	Sometimes, it is necessary to refer to organizational units, or individual locations, email addresses, or telephone numbers. In these cases, reconfirm their validity every time the policy is reviewed.

Table 16.1: Suggestions for Inclusion into a Data Policy Style Guide

The suggestions in Table 16.1 may or may not fit a particular enterprise. However, they highlight the need to develop a Policy Style Guide, as there are many ways in which confusion and inconsistency can arise when writing data policies.

Use the Policy Style Guide during policy formulation. As such, it is more of a standard than a guide. However, some discretion must always be allowed to conform to the overall principles for writing data policies.

The Policy Style Guide should be reviewed annually by the Data Policy Operations Committee to make sure that it is still fully relevant. If an update is required, it will need to be approved by the Data Policy Oversight Committee.

Chapter 17

Data Policy Harmonization

In the wider world, policy harmonization is the process to ensure that different policies do not contradict or duplicate each other. Large organizations like governments and multinational companies with many different departments usually need it. For data policies, we have some advantages based on the approaches recommended in this book that help reduce, but not eliminate, the need for policy harmonization, specifically:

- A single set of principles to which data policies are aligned.

- A well-defined data policy lifecycle.

- A single organizational body, the Data Policy Oversight Committee, to ensure the good development of all data policies.

It almost goes without saying that one policy statement in a data policy must not conflict with another policy statement in the same policy. The guidance we have given should avoid that. However, in very verbose "blob of text" policies, there is a real possibility of such conflict, or the appearance of it, because of lack of clarity.

But even with our approach of structured policy statements there is always a risk that one data policy could be incompatible in some way with another data policy or even a non-data policy. We need to address this risk.

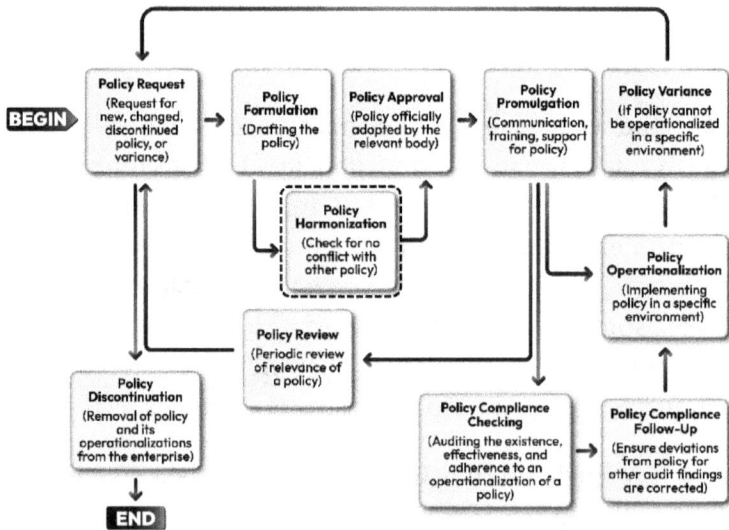

Figure 17.1: Policy Harmonization in the Policy Lifecycle

Policy Harmonization Process

Some larger enterprises have a dedicated policy harmonization unit. Submitting a draft policy to this unit for review before approval will be part of the policy lifecycle. The policy harmonization unit will match the policy statements and terminology we use in all other policies across the enterprise. Some degree of automated search can be used to do this, but often the staff of the unit have good working knowledge of all the policies and do the work manually.

In most enterprises, however, there is not a policy harmonization unit, but the policy harmonization check must still be carried out for data policies. The best way to perform the checks is to give the draft policy to staff in the Data Governance unit who are familiar with all data policies, but who were not involved in drafting the policy to be reviewed. Of course, the team that drafted the policy should certainly examine other data policies for their statements and terminology. Even so, it is very difficult for people to spot their own mistakes, and it is better to ask people with a fresh outlook to review the draft policy.

A policy harmonization review should be just that. Do not use it to question the need for the policy or particular policy statements. All it should do is ensure the policy statements are not incompatible with statements in other data policies, and that the terminology is also aligned unless there are special requirements for the terminology in the policy under review.

Dealing with Inconsistencies

Send back any inconsistencies detected due to the policy harmonization process to the team that drafted the policy for correction. Hopefully, this will not involve any significant issues and will be more of a case of adjusting language.

However, if there are significant issues, the policy formulation working group will need to deal with them.

Just because the draft policy is inconsistent with another policy does not mean the draft policy is wrong. It may be that the other policy is at fault. If the policy formulation team feels there is a problem with another policy, they need to raise a policy request to get the other policy changed. Doing this may take a while, but any alternative is much worse. Generally, policy work is rarely fast because policies have wide impact and must be developed carefully.

If the draft policy has problems, and these are material, it will have to be redrafted by the formulation team. This may require going through the stakeholder consultation process again.

After correcting any issues with the draft policy, send it back for another policy harmonization review.

Data Policies vs. Non-Data Policies

So far, we have considered organizations with either:

- A dedicated policy harmonization unit for all policies.

- Organizations that lack such a unit, but have a process to ensure harmonization of a draft data policy with other data policies.

This still leaves open the possibility that a draft data policy may be incompatible with some other policy that is not a data policy. A reasonable way to deal with such a possibility is to send the draft policy for review to other business units that are likely to have policies that may have indirect links to data, for example:

- Legal (because of data privacy and contractual aspects of licensed data).

- Risk (because Risk operates at a higher level).

- IT (because IT deals with technology that processes data).

- Enterprise Architecture (because Data Architecture is generally part of this unit).

- Procurement (if the purchase of data is involved).

There may be other organizational units, too.

Data Governance needs to be clear that the only request of these other units is to review the policy and determine if there are any inconsistencies with the policies for which the other units are responsible. These other units must not be given a veto on or question the draft policy. They should have been asked to participate in the stakeholder review during policy formulation if they needed to be more closely involved.

If an inconsistency is found between a data policy and a non-data policy as part of these reviews, then Data Governance will need to coordinate with the other organizational unit(s) to settle the differences. While this may be a significant effort, it is far less than will be involved if the data policy gets promulgated and the inconsistencies are found later.

Figure 17.2 illustrates the overall process.

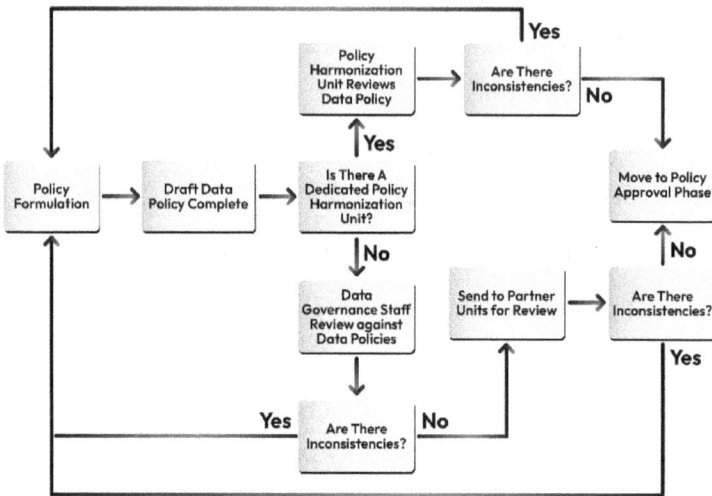

Figure 17.2: High Level Summary of Policy Harmonization Process

Policy Coordination

One step beyond policy harmonization with non-data policies is policy coordination. This is where Data Governance involves other organizational units like Legal, Risk, etc., who are informed of the state of the data policy portfolio and can express any views about it. Sometimes, staff from these units are included as members of the Data Policy Oversight Committee. If that is not the case, achieve policy coordination by circulating the minutes of the Data Policy Oversight Committee to the other units and allowing staff from them to attend meetings in observer status (not as voting members).

Likewise, these other units can inform Data Governance of their policy initiatives, and Data Governance can provide feedback to them.

The advantage of this approach is that it benefits the enterprise as a whole, and issues can be uncovered and dealt with before the policy harmonization phase. It requires a persistent vision to do policy work well, and a constant effort to work with other organizational units to achieve this vision. The effort is well worth it, and Data Governance units that develop good working relationships with other units will be seen as an asset to the enterprise.

Finalizing Policy Harmonization

We have seen that there can be four possible outcomes of this phase of the policy lifecycle:

- There are no harmonization issues, in which case the policy can proceed to policy approval, and the Policy Administrator can update the Policy Portfolio to show that the policy harmonization step is complete.

- There are issues with the policy and the draft has to be amended. In this case, the policy has to go back to the policy formulation working group to be updated. The policy formulation phase has to be repeated.

- The draft has no issues, but another data policy has issues. A new policy request is raised to deal with this second data policy. The Policy Administrator will have to request the Data Policy Oversight Committee to put the current policy on hold until the policy request for the second policy is processed. Then both policies can be promulgated simultaneously.

- The draft has no issues, but a non-data policy has issues. The Policy Administrator will have to request the Data Policy Oversight Committee to put the current policy on hold while Data Governance negotiates with the organizational unit that owns the second data policy. The Data Policy Oversight Committee can only release its hold on the current policy when there is a resolution.

Obviously, it is best never to get into a situation where harmonization issues occur, which is yet another reason for being very careful when doing policy work.

## Chapter 18

Data Policy Approval

Following policy harmonization, we are now ready to get our draft policy finally approved. Earlier, the Data Policy Oversight Committee approved the draft to move forward to policy harmonization, but now final approval is needed. Of course, it is not just drafts of new policies that need approval but also policy updates and discontinuation of policies. However, to simplify the discussion, we will follow the example of the formulation of a new policy.

"Approval" means the policy is ready to be promulgated and operationalized.

The reasons for having an approval step are:

- To ensure there is management oversight of data policies.
- To provide a final check to ensure the substantive content of a policy has no issues.

- To provide a final check on the format and style of the policy.
- Approval for next steps with the policy, including promulgation and effective dates.
- To ensure that the processes of the policy lifecycle have been followed and there is no "rogue" policy development.
- To ensure any needed coordination with other areas of the enterprise has been or is being undertaken.
- To track progress against the overall plans for data policies.
- To catch any issues that are management responsibilities, like shortage of resources.
- To officially disband any working group connected with policy formulation.

There may also be additional, more specific reasons that matter to a particular enterprise.

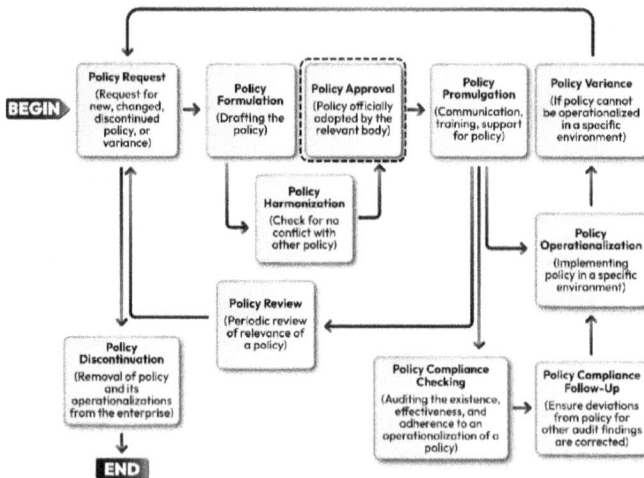

Figure 18.1: Policy Approval in The Policy Lifecycle

Who Approves a Data Policy?

Clearly, the Data Policy Oversight Committee is one point of approval in the structure we propose. The committee has ultimate responsibility for all data policies and so needs to ensure every policy is of an acceptable quality. A policy cannot move forward in the policy lifecycle unless this initial approval step is completed. As we have discussed previously, the committee will approve the final draft at the end of the policy formulation phase.

In general, the committee will need to meet to vote on approving a new policy. This is because there are a lot of points to be checked for a new policy. By contrast, a minor change to an existing policy may not require a meeting, and voting members of the committee could vote via email or some equivalent mechanism. This reduces wait times for such minor changes and eases the burden of committee meetings. Any option for voting outside of a meeting will need to be specified in the policy of policies. Perhaps some flexibility can be allowed for the chair to permit approvals of minimal changes via email.

More importantly, in many organizations, there is an overall policy lifecycle beyond what might be established for data policies that requires policies to be approved by one or more other bodies. This is particularly true in heavily regulated industries like finance and pharmaceuticals.

Some enterprises with multiple approval points may have even more complex arrangements. Perhaps there is a more technical lower-level body like a Risk Sub-committee that must approve a policy action before it goes to an ultimate higher-level body.

These other bodies will provide approval after the policy harmonization phase, whereas the Data Policy Oversight Committee provides approval prior to the policy harmonization phase.

Preparing for Approval

The Policy Administrator is responsible for shepherding the draft policy through the approval process. This individual must be familiar with how the Data Policy Oversight Committee works, including how it conducts business, what matters to members, what does not, and what reading matter must be produced ahead of time. Nobody should be assigned to the role of Policy Administrator until they have attended enough of the committee's meetings to become familiar with its workings. Of course, at the outset, when the committee is just starting, this will not be possible, and Policy Administrators simply have to do the best they can until they understand how the committee works.

The situation is different with other approval bodies. The worst thing a Policy Administrator can do is simply send the draft policy to them for approval and wait to see what happens. Proper relations have to be established, and since units outside of Data Governance are involved, establishing such relations is the responsibility of the Data Governance Lead.

Assuming the additional approval body is a committee, the Data Governance Lead must contact the chair and committee secretary to find out how it works. The Data Governance Lead represents the Data Governance unit to all outside business units, so it is his or her task to do this. Contact should be made long before any policy action is sent for approval. The Data Governance Lead will have to explain what the Data Governance unit is, what data policies are, and what the Data Policy Oversight Committee is. Conversely, the Data Governance Lead will have to learn as much as possible about how the approval body operates, not just the formal processes but also the personal dynamics involved. If this sounds a little political, it is. Once good relations are established, Policy Administrators can deal with policy actions going to these approval bodies.

Ideally, the Data Governance Lead will gather sufficient situational awareness of each approval body to make it easy for Policy Administrators to work with it. The mechanisms to send data policy actions for approval should be understood, as well as how to confirm approval has been granted. This last point is important. For example, some committees can vote for approval in a meeting, but their charter explicitly states that approval is not granted until it appears in published minutes. Policy Administrators need to understand all these nuances.

When it comes to the Policy Administrator sending policy actions to an approval body, it may sometimes be wise to meet personally with the chair and interested members prior to any meeting to explain the policy action. This will reduce any time wasted in explanations during committee meetings by better informing the chair and members who do not have the background that the Data Policy Oversight

Committee has. It is also likely to increase the chances of approval.

We have been considering an approval body beyond the Data Governance Management Committee as being a committee, but sometimes it may be an individual, such as an executive. However, the same approach can be used.

What Gets Approved?

Let us go back to the point in time when the Data Policy Oversight Committee had to approve the policy draft or other policy action. There are other things that the committee should at least review and, in some cases, approve:

- Were all the required procedures followed? The committee needs to at least state in the minutes that it accepts this was done.

- Did the stakeholder review include any significant resistance to the policy, and has this been dealt with? Again, the minutes must capture that the committee is satisfied.

- Does the committee approve the draft? A vote is needed for approval.

- Does the committee approve the policy promulgation plan? We have not discussed promulgation yet, but we will consider this point further in the next chapter.

- Does the committee approve the dates for when promulgation will occur and when the policy will begin to be enforced? Again, we will discuss promulgation more in the next chapter. The committee may or may not vote on this point, but must clearly state the dates are approved in the minutes.

- If one or more other approval bodies exist in the enterprise, the committee has to approve that the draft will be submitted to these bodies. Again, this must be stated in the minutes.

In some enterprises, additional items may need to be approved.

The minutes of the meeting are proof of all approvals by the committee. The Policy Administrator can update the Policy Portfolio for the policy involved once the minutes are published.

At this point, the approval of the Data Policy Oversight Committee has been obtained. The policy harmonization phase can now be undertaken, and if successful, the policy can be sent to any other bodies in the enterprise for review. There should be no need to come back to the Data Policy Oversight Committee after approvals have been obtained from these other bodies, but the members of the committee should be made aware of progress. If one of the other approval bodies refuses to approve the policy, it should be brought back to the Data Policy Oversight Committee to decide the next steps. This is clearly an exceptional situation, so it may not be amenable to a prescribed procedure, and the committee will need to decide what to do on a case-by-case basis.

Disbanding the Working Group

Once the Data Policy Oversight Committee has approved a draft new or updated policy, there is usually no longer any need for the working group that produced the draft. However, issues may arise during consideration by any higher-level approval bodies. So, the working group should be disbanded only after obtaining all approvals, which should be the normal course of events. The Data Policy Oversight Committee can conditionally approve the disbandment of the working group after final approval is obtained, and the Policy Administrator can be directed to inform the members of the working group when this happens, and notify the committee at its next meeting thereafter. The disbandment will be noted in the minutes of that meeting.

It is a good practice for as many members of the working group as possible to attend the Data Policy Oversight Committee meeting when requesting approval so that they can answer any questions from committee members.

> *It is also good practice for the committee to thank the working group members for their efforts. The chair of the committee can also send messages of gratitude to the managers of the working group participants who are not Data Governance staff.*

This is significant since participating in policy working groups is voluntary.

Updating the Policy Portfolio

At each point where an approval is obtained, the Policy Administrator must update the Policy Portfolio with the decision, the body that made the decision, the date of the decision, and any relevant details. The status of the policy must also be updated. This ensures that the status of the policy in the Policy Portfolio is always accurate.

The names of the members of the working group who drafted the new policy must also be recorded, as they may need to be consulted in the future.

Conclusion

Policy approval is perhaps the policy lifecycle phase with the most institutional participation. The initial approval by the Data Policy Oversight Committee at the end of policy formulation and the higher-level approvals following policy harmonization require the Policy Administrator to be careful about satisfying each approval body's requirements and ensuring good coordination. Without this, there is the possibility of lengthy delays in the overall approval step, which can impact the operationalization of the policy. Good administrative practices and attention to detail are particularly important to make this phase go smoothly and have the policy ready for promulgation according to schedule.

## Chapter 19

Data Policy Promulgation

Promulgation traditionally means to publicly proclaim a new law or edict to a population. While ignorance of the law is no excuse in a courtroom, governments have traditionally tried to make sure that the governed know what laws are on the books. The same holds true for policies in enterprises.

> *Everyone subject to a policy is supposed to abide by it, but it can sometimes be difficult for staff to be aware of new or changed policies.*

Therefore, it is necessary to make an effort to promulgate policies. Communication is a vital area that is too often overlooked in Data Governance units, particularly those focusing on technical aspects of data. Policy promulgation is much easier for Data Governance units with well-developed communication capabilities. Even then, there are some unique features that are not encountered in general communications.

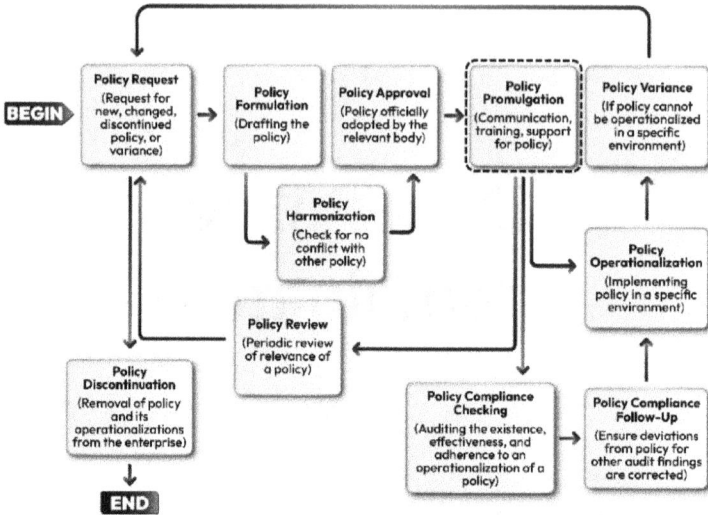

Figure 19.1: Policy Promulgation in the Policy Lifecycle

What Has to be Communicated

The basic facts to communicate for policy actions are:

- **New Policy:** An overview of the new policy, when it will come into force, and the text of the policy itself.

- **Changed Policy:** A summary of the changes, when the changes take effect, and the text of the changes.

- **Discontinued Policy:** A notice of discontinuation, when the discontinuation takes effect, and a description of any policy that replaces the discontinued policy.

Even for the basic facts, we can see that two broad categories of information need to be communicated. One is the text of the policy itself, and the other is the announcement of a policy action. We will now consider the communication requirements for each of these categories.

Where to Publish a Policy

Obviously, the decision of where to publish data policies should be taken during the formulation of the policy of policies, long before arriving at the point of any policy promulgation. Policies used to be distributed in printed form, but today, policies are usually housed online. For data policies, there are two main alternatives:

- **Enterprise Policy Site:** All data policies are co-located on a single enterprise-wide intranet site, along with all the other policies of the enterprise. This site is under the control of a centralized group, such as Risk.

- **Data Governance Site:** In this alternative, all data policies are housed in an intranet site that is exclusively for the use of Data Governance and is controlled by Data Governance.

There can be variations of these themes. For instance, conglomerates of distinct operating companies, very large companies with sizable departments, and multinational corporations operating in different countries may have intranet sites at the operating company, department, and country level, respectively.

For Data Governance, publishing data policies on an intranet site it controls is operationally the easiest solution as the Data Governance unit can do this independently. On the other hand, having all enterprise policies in one online site is easier for staff, as it reduces the need to search. However, Data Governance then has to coordinate publication with the unit that controls the site.

Obviously, a compromise is to have an enterprise-wide site with a link for data policies to a site that Data Governance controls. Even this may require negotiation and approval at the executive level before it can be implemented. All of this has to be sorted out as the policy of policies is being developed.

If Data Governance has to use an enterprise-wide site, then no further design work is required for the publication of policies. All Data Governance needs to know is the process for getting policies published on the enterprise-wide site. This must include an understanding of how long it takes for publication.

However, if Data Governance controls the intranet site on which policies are published, there is much more work that Data Governance will have to do.

Posting a Data Policy on an Intranet Site

A dedicated data policy intranet site will obviously have to list the data policies, with links to each policy. The policy titles should be self-explanatory, but the site can also repeat the policy description information element next to each policy title. This is the same description that is found in the policy document itself. It is very important that nothing on the intranet site differs from what is found in the policies in any way, as this could be open to a different interpretation than the policy itself.

With respect to the policies, they can be directly embedded as HTML text on individual pages, or each policy can be a document, such as a PDF document that is opened via a link to it. The advantages of the document approach are:

- No new intranet pages are required when a new policy needs to be added.

- The document can be downloaded, printed, and studied, providing more flexibility.

- The document can be stored in a secure location with restricted update access, helping ensure data policies are not tampered with.

- The policy will be drafted and approved as a document, and keeping it as a document means there is no transfer of the text to a web page, which might result in errors.

- The document can be hashed, such as via SHA-256 to produce a hash key, which can be reproduced at any time and compared to the original SHA-256 value to confirm authenticity.

Different enterprises have different viewpoints on how policies in production should be stored, but the linked document approach seems to be the best.

One of the first steps in policy promulgation is to get the policy onto the intranet site where it needs to be housed and to prove that it can be accessed without any issue. It is the task of the Policy Administrator to ensure this is done. For a site managed by Data Governance, there will usually be a single administrator who has to perform the update. For an enterprise-level site, some other unit will need to be requested to post the policy.

The Policy Bulletin

The intranet site to house the policies is not the only piece of infrastructure that will be needed in the promulgation of data policies. If we look once again at how governments promulgate laws passed by legislatures, we will find that most of them have some form of periodical that they use to publish laws and regulations, or deliberative proceedings. For instance, the US Federal Government has The Federal Register, and the UK government has Hansard.

When it comes to data policies, we will have many new policies, plus some revisions and some discontinuations. If all these policy actions get communicated individually then staff will not be able to easily find out the totality of all the policy actions that have occurred in a given timeframe. For instance, if every time there is a policy action, all that happens is an email sent to the entire enterprise with details of that policy action alone, staff will not be able to understand the history of changes for the policy. Centuries ago in Europe, Town Criers and Heralds were employed by the government to go to towns and villages and read out loud individual laws and proclamations. This was necessary given the largely illiterate citizenry, but usually, the text of only one law was being delivered. This piecemeal method is no better than our standalone emails for each policy action.

A better approach is to emulate what modern governments do and have what we will call a "Policy Bulletin."

This is a list of all data policy actions in date sequence with the most recent at the top. Perhaps more properly, it should be called the "Data Policy Bulletin," but for ease of reference in this book, we will simply call it the "Policy Bulletin."

It is important to keep the Policy Bulletin simple to make it easier to read, and the information elements should include:

- Name of the data policy. This should also be a link to the policy.

- Type of policy action (new, updated, discontinued).

- A description of the policy action. For new policies, this should be the same description that occurs in the policy. For policy updates, it should be a summary of the changes. For policy discontinuations, it should be the rationale for why the policy is being discontinued plus identification of any policy that is replacing it.

- The effective date of the policy action. That is, when it comes into force.

- The date the item was published in the Policy Bulletin.

From this list, it is easy to see that the Policy Bulletin should be in a tabular format. Ideally, it will be maintained as a database table, or a table in a data catalog or SaaS software. If necessary, it could be an Excel spreadsheet. It needs to be published in a tabular report format on the intranet site where the policies are housed. Figure 19.2 illustrates the architecture.

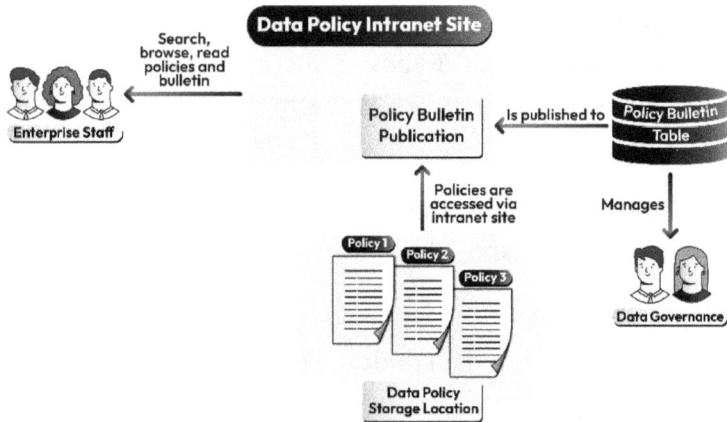

Figure 19.2: Summary Architecture for Data Policies and Data Bulletin

The link to the policy will lead directly to the text of the policy, which, as discussed previously, should be a document. Alternatively, the link could lead to the intranet page that has the entire list of data policies. The user would then have to click again on the specific policy to access its text. The advantage of the former approach is fewer clicks. Still, the advantage of the latter approach is that the user sees a list of all data policies and has easier access to navigation around the relevant intranet pages.

General Promulgation Actions

With the policy text put on an intranet page and the Policy Bulletin updated with the latest policy actions, the next promulgation activities can start.

Data Governance should find out if there is any process for informing staff about policy actions that apply generally. If there is, then updates about data policies will simply have to follow this process. A single promulgation process at the enterprise level for all policies makes sense, since staff can get confused if they receive messages about different policies in different formats from different areas of the organization.

Unfortunately, there are many enterprises where this level of coordination does not exist, and in these cases, Data Governance is on its own. There are three basic ways in which Data Governance can broadly communicate policy actions:

- Emails to everyone in the enterprise who needs to be aware of the policy action. The new policy actions should be displayed in the email as they appear in the Policy Bulletin and the email should have a link to the Policy Bulletin.

- A prominent banner on the corporate intranet home page that announces there are policy changes and links to the Policy Bulletin.

- Messaging via whatever corporate messaging software is used. A message that there have been policy updates, and a link to the Policy Bulletin are sufficient.

> *Today, these communication techniques are less effective than in the past as the channels involved are all saturated.*

Leadership and corporate communications seem to put out messages every day, many of which are of questionable usefulness for staff in carrying out their duties. The result is that the staff are overwhelmed with information and cannot easily determine what applies to them and what does not. Nevertheless, Data Governance will have to use one or more of these channels. Sending multiple messages for a given set of policy actions is probably not a good idea, as it may annoy staff to the point where they immediately ignore the messages.

To the extent possible, all broad communications sent out by Data Governance to promulgate new policy actions should be coordinated with any other unit of the enterprise that also does broad communications. Recall that we are discussing the situation where there is no corporate mechanism for promulgating policies generally, and that Data Governance has to do its own promulgation. Even in this situation, there may still be some kind of framework for general communications that has to be followed. Perhaps it is controlled by Corporate Communications, Human Resources, or some staff working closely with the executive level. Data Governance must try to find out if there is anyone who has accountability for broad communications in the enterprise and try to work with them. At a minimum, Data Governance should be able to send out its policy communications when it knows there are no other important communications being delivered to the enterprise, which might take attention away from anything Data Governance sends out.

Targeted Promulgation Actions

Broad communications of data policy actions are needed in part because of fairness. Everyone in the enterprise should have a reasonable chance of finding out about new policy actions. However, Data Governance can also deliver more targeted communications to promulgate policy actions. This makes sense as some staff are more closely connected than others when working with data or interacting with Data Governance.

Targeted Data Governance communications are also a good idea because the units and individual staff members who work closely with data and Data Governance will likely expect to hear about policy changes before other staff. This is also because they may be questioned about the changes and want to be prepared. Some of the groups who should be considered for targeted communications are:

- **Internal Audit and any other internal function that checks policy compliance.** Obviously, these groups need to understand what the policy actions entail and prepare for how to check them. Data Governance should consider working with these groups as soon as approval has been obtained for a policy action, which may take a considerable time before any general communication goes out.

- **Data Governance Partners.** These are organizational units that Data Governance has close links with and leverages to help in its work. Examples include Legal, IT, Risk, and Enterprise Architecture. As partners, such units expect to hear important communications about data matters before anyone else. Data Governance also has the opportunity to explain in detail the rationale and history of policy actions so that these units have a deeper understanding of them. Note that this relationship should also work in reverse. Data Governance should expect to be informed of policy actions these other units take before they send any broad communications.

- **Data Stewards.** Exactly what Data Stewards are and what they do is a highly debated topic, but to some extent, they champion the ideal of good data management and have close links with the Data Governance unit. Data Governance can send them information about the new policy actions and when to expect broad communications about them. In this way, the Data Stewards can prepare themselves and the areas in which they work.

An important point for targeted communications is that the individuals being targeted must be clearly known to Data Governance.

There should not be any guesswork in this regard. Staff who receive targeted communications about new data policy actions but have little involvement with data or Data Governance may get very confused. Therefore, granular lists of individuals to be targeted should be maintained. Data Governance units with well-developed communications capabilities should have such lists. The Data Policy Operations Committee should create them if they do not exist.

Because targeted communications are much more limited in scale, they can be more personalized. For instance, Data Governance staff can meet with groups to deliver a presentation on the new policy actions, and answer questions about the policy actions. The content of meetings is far more likely to be remembered than emails, and the individuals in the audience are much more likely to be motivated to behave as influencers promoting awareness of the policy actions to other staff.

Promulgation Planning

From the above discussion, it is easy to understand that policy promulgation can take a lot of effort, and that some measures can be more effective than others. It is a good idea to develop a detailed plan for policy promulgation so that all the steps can be coordinated and executed in a timely manner. An approval body may sometimes want to see such a plan, particularly if complex policies are involved. It may even be necessary to get approval for a promulgation plan in addition to policy actions.

Training

While promulgation is fundamentally concerned with communication, there may sometimes need to be training for policies. As we have discussed before, a policy should not include any training material, but training may be needed, particularly when a policy introduces a new concept. For instance, some years ago Data Privacy policies were quickly introduced into many organizations. Previously, few people had cared about Data Privacy, and many people thought it was the same as Data Security. The only way to solve this issue was to provide training in the concept of Data Privacy and its practical implications.

Policy training can be as simple as delivering a presentation online and recording the presentation. The recording can then be made available to staff via the communications sent out for general promulgation.

Promulgation Log

A final point on promulgation is that all the data policy communications that are delivered should be recorded in a single central log. This can provide evidence for auditors or regulators of adequate efforts to promulgate a policy action. The log can also be used to derive metrics about the level and efficiency of promulgation. It can be a spreadsheet, a table in a SaaS database product, or a configured asset in a data catalog. Once again, this metadata is a simple but important list. The Policy Inventory can also be updated following promulgation to reflect the completion of this phase of the policy lifecycle.

Chapter 20

Data Policy
Operationalization

So far, we have been considering data policies mainly from the viewpoint of centralized organizational bodies, such as Data Governance.

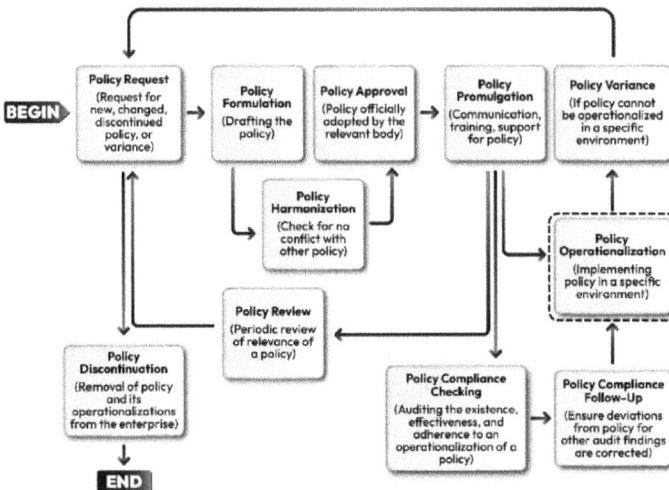

Figure 20.1: Policy Operationalization in the Policy Lifecycle

Once a policy is promulgated, however, it goes into the general enterprise where it is now up to individuals and business units to operationalize.

Non-Operationalization

A business unit must examine a data policy to see if it applies to them. Since data is used practically everywhere, there is a high probability that most data policies will apply to any business unit, but there can be some data policies that do not.

> If a business unit determines that a data policy does not apply, it should document the fact with reasoning.

Unfortunately, most business units do not do this, although they are more likely to do so in highly regulated industries. Any solution to this problem, like forcing documentation of non-applicability of a policy, will have to apply to all policies and therefore need to come from the executive level, or a department like Risk, which has the authority to deal with the issue.

In this regard, Data Governance should deal carefully with all non-data policies that it has to comply with. If there is a policy from Finance that does not apply to Data Governance, then Data Governance should formally document the fact that it does not apply and the reasons. As a policy-setting unit, Data Governance must be very fastidious in its compliance with all policies that do or do not apply to it. Otherwise, people will take notice and Data Governance will lose valuable prestige, impacting the success of its policy efforts.

Operationalization Support

While it is up to individuals and units in the enterprise to operationalize a data policy if it applies to them, not all these individuals and units may know how to do it.

Operationalization requires a significant understanding of the processes that an individual or organizational unit carries out to design an operationalization solution. However, not everyone may fully understand the policy, no matter how well it is written, how well policy promulgation is carried out, and what additional services Data Governance may provide like training.

If an organizational unit does not think it fully understands a data policy, it is going to contact Data Governance using the support email address that is in the policy. Data Governance will have to respond to the specific questions that the unit has.

It might seem like a good idea for Data Governance to prepare additional material about a policy, like FAQs, to reduce the policy's support load. However, this can make things worse, as organizational units can then have questions about the FAQs. Also, the FAQs can be interpreted in ways that differ from the policy, no matter how illogical these interpretations are, by organizational units who can then think they can evade the policy.

Furthermore, an organizational unit may have questions that require explaining the specifics of their processes, which is not something any FAQ produced by Data Governance can cover.

It is better, therefore, for Data Governance to provide support for data policies directly to organizational units that request it. Data Governance should limit its support to helping with interpretation and understanding of the policy in question. It should not design, help to design, or approve the design of whatever procedures are put in place to operationalize the policy. Data Governance cannot do that because it cannot know enough about the processes of the organizational unit involved. Nor can Data Governance assess and affirm compliance of any organizational unit. That requires a separation of duties, with Internal Audit or some other objective verification mechanism being used to assess compliance.

Tracking Support Requests

Support requests will provide an indication of difficulties the enterprise is having with the data policy. Therefore, it is a good idea to track the support requests that come in and the resolutions provided. Ticketing software, like that used by IT help desks, may be available to Data Governance. Alternatively, the same software solutions discussed previously for metadata can be leveraged, such as spreadsheets, SaaS software, and data catalogs.

It is important to document the resolutions provided as they can be reused for any similar support requests.

Another insight to glean from support requests is whether a particular organizational unit keeps having operational difficulties across a range of policies. Such a finding may indicate the need for data literacy training or setting up more data stewards in these units. Figure 20.2 summarizes the policy operationalization process from the perspective of Data Governance.

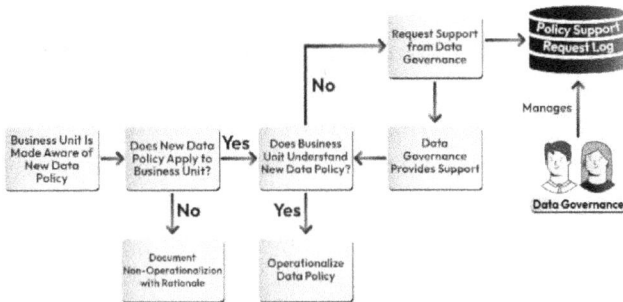

Figure 20.2: High Level Summary of Policy Operationalization

Preparing for Data Policy Administration

Another set of tasks for Data Governance at policy operationalization time is preparing for steady-state policy administration. The earlier phases of the policy lifecycle up to and including policy promulgation focus on developing policies, requiring scheduled and dedicated time.

> The remaining phases may well be a lot quieter, with mostly only occasional work involved and perhaps a few intensive periods.

It may be that different staff members in Data Governance are more suited to each of these parts of the policy lifecycle so that during policy operationalization, there is a transition of responsibility for a policy to a new staff person. Alternatively, the same individual can continue as the Policy Administrator. The choice is dependent on how Data Governance wishes to organize itself.

Strategy for Policy Operationalization

We can clearly see that several considerations come into play during policy operationalization. The tasks that Data Governance needs to perform during policy operationalization should not be a set of *ad hoc* activities that are done differently each time a new or updated policy gets implemented. Everyone in Data Governance should know what is required and how to get it done. If this is not the case, there is a strong possibility that units in the general enterprise that have to operationalize the policy will not be well supported, and compliance will be inadequate.

Given this, it is worthwhile for Data Governance to think in detail about its strategy for policy operationalization when developing the policy of policies. In particular, Data Governance may need to estimate the level of resources required to adequately support the operationalization of data policies. This point is often overlooked, and Data Governance units can find themselves having difficulty in providing adequate support. Remember that policy support activities may increase as more and more data policies are issued. A good approach is to track the trends in policy support activities in order to project future support needs. Additional resources for Data Governance can then be justifiably requested.

## Chapter 21

Data Policy Variances

Policy variances are permissions for noncompliance with all or a part of a data policy that are granted for a limited period of time to an organizational unit that would otherwise have to comply fully with the policy. Sometimes they are called "policy exceptions," but we prefer the term "policy variance" because "policy exception" can give the impression that permission has been granted to never comply with the policy. Other people think a "policy exception" is a finding of noncompliance, which is even more confusing. "Policy variance" is a little closer to the concept of permission to temporarily delay the full operationalization of a policy.

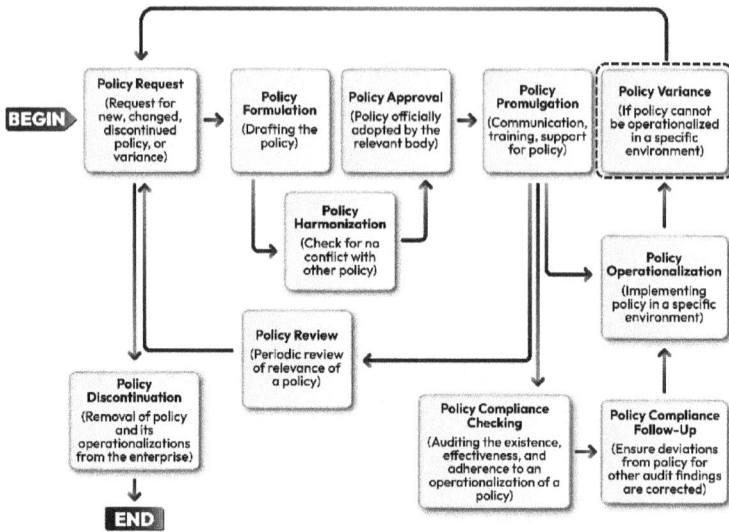

Figure 21.1: Policy Variances in the Policy Lifecycle

Reason for Policy Variances

In the chapter on policy operationalization, we discussed the situation of an organizational unit that determines a data policy does not apply to it and recommended that the unit document the fact that the policy does not apply to it, together with the rationale.

> *What we are discussing in this chapter is an organizational unit that determines that a data policy does apply to it, but the unit is not currently in a position to fully operationalize the policy.*

As an example, a data science unit may be using datasets that contain very old data, but which are needed for historical trend analysis. A new data retention policy may require these old datasets to be deleted. However, because the data science unit uses so many of them, it may be difficult to locate all the datasets and adjust the data pipelines and models that use them. Therefore, the data science unit may request a variance to allow it more time to comply with the policy.

The situation we want to avoid is that an organizational unit simply ignores the data policy in these circumstances. Unfortunately, this happens in many organizations where Data Governance just focuses on formulating data policies and does not pay attention to the rest of the policy lifecycle. Since Data Governance often cannot know with certainty which organizational units must comply with a data policy and which organizational units it does not apply to, Data Governance cannot easily identify situations where the policy applies, but the policy is being ignored.

Policy variances solve this problem because they force an organizational unit to submit a request for approval of temporary noncompliance with a data policy rather than just ignoring it. With policy variances, Data Governance knows exactly who has problems with operationalizing a policy.

Mandate for Policy Variances

Before designing how variances will work for data policies, Data Governance should first find out if variances are used in any other policy context in the enterprise. It may be that there is already a well-established set of procedures for policy variances, and if this is the case, Data Governance simply needs to adopt these procedures.

Perhaps there are no enterprise-wide policy variance procedures, but some policy areas, like Human Resources, have developed their own variance procedures. Data Governance should at least do enough due diligence to identify any best practices and lessons learned in these areas. Clearly, these practices are not mandated for Data Governance, but they may contain elements worth copying.

Assuming there are no mandated processes for policy variances, Data Governance can design how variances for data policies should be handled. This must be done during the formulation of the policy of policies, which must cover variances. The policy of policies must include provisions that require policy variances to be submitted as policy requests to Data Governance if a data policy cannot be operationalized or otherwise complied with, in whole or in part. This is one part of the data policy of policies that applies to the entire enterprise, not just to Data Governance.

The Data Policy Variance Procedure

The procedure to submit a request for a data policy variance must be simple and easy to do. It must be very formal, as formality ensures a level playing field for all, with no special privileges for some, and formality adds to the seriousness of requesting a variance, which is an action that should not be usual.

The best approach is to have an organizational unit requesting a variance fill out a form and submit it to Data Governance. This Policy Variance Request Form can be part of a workflow or it can be processed manually. It should contain:

- The name of the submitting organizational unit.

- The name of the policy.

- Identification of specific parts of the policy that cannot be complied with (or stating that the policy cannot be complied with in its entirety).

- The reasons for requesting a variance.

- An indication of when the policy will be complied with by the organizational unit.

- The period for which the variance is being requested. This cannot be more than six months.

- Any additional information.

- The name and email of the manager of the organizational unit requesting the variance.

- The name and email of the person submitting the variance request.

The Policy Registrar will process the form once it is received by Data Governance. The form will be treated as another type of policy request and in generally the same way as other policy requests, but with the following differences:

- The Policy Registrar will acknowledge receipt of the form back to both the submitter and manager of the organizational unit making the request. This will be done within 24 hours of receiving the request.

- The email back to the manager and submitter will state that the organizational unit does not have to comply with whatever part of the data policy was described in the request until the Data Policy Oversight Committee considers the request. It is important not to leave any uncertainly about compliance in any part of the variance procedure. Since the organizational unit is not complying anyway, permission might as well be given temporarily.

- The email back to the manager and submitter will provide a link to documentation of the procedure to process the variance request and the timeframes involved. There is no guarantee that the staff of the organizational unit have a detailed understanding of the variance procedure.

- The email back to the manager and submitter will state that the Policy Administrator for the policy concerned is now the point of contact for the organizational unit for following up on the variance request.

The Policy Registrar will update the Policy Request Log with the request. The date the request was received will be treated as the start date for all subsequent time periods connected with the variance request. The Policy Registrar must inform the Policy Administrator for the policy in question about the variance request. The Policy Administrator must follow up with the requesting unit to determine if the request is simply due to a lack of understanding of the policy or is somehow trivial. If, as a result of this, the requesting unit comes to understand that a variance is not needed, then the Policy Administrator can inform the Policy Registrar and the variance can be closed out in the Policy Request Log.

If the Policy Administrator agrees that the requesting unit understands the policy and the request is not trivial, then the variance request must continue to the Data Policy Oversight Committee with the Policy Administrator's notes on the detailed situation involved.

Consideration of the Variance Request

Variance requests need to be considered by the Data Policy Oversight Committee, and should be moved ahead of all other policy requests so they are considered at the first meeting of the committee following their receipt. If the Policy Registrar receives an unusually large number of variance requests, they should inform the secretary of the committee, who can then discuss with the chair the possibility of an extraordinary meeting of the committee. It is also possible that committee members can consider variances via email, but this will need to be stated in the policy of policies.

Variance requests should be unusual. During policy formulation, one of the steps was stakeholder consultation, which should have indicated any likelihood of widespread difficulty operationalizing the policy.

The policy formulation process should have adjusted the policy to rectify any such operationalization difficulties.

When considering the variance request, the committee should request the attendance of someone who can represent the organizational unit involved and provide more details about the difficulties the unit is having. The request should be denied if the organizational unit cannot send anyone.

In general, the committee should always approve the first variance request for a particular policy from an organizational unit for three months. If the unit states that it simply needs time to work on operationalization, then the situation will be fairly straightforward. Perhaps such variance requests could even be automatically approved without the need for committee consideration. The policy of policies could reflect such an approach.

It is possible that an organizational unit submits a variance request to never comply with the policy, or submits a second request for a continuation of a variance for a policy, or it cannot provide a clear timeline for operationalization.. In these circumstances there is a bigger problem, and the committee must direct the Policy Administrator to investigate the situation and report back. It may be the case that the Policy Administrator has to get help from other staff in Data Governance to complete the work.

One month should be allowed for the investigation, and the Policy Administrator must report back at the next committee meeting thereafter. The variance can be approved for this one-month period. One month may seem like a short time, but it is important that out-of-compliance conditions are not allowed to persist. Data policies exist for many reasons, but risk management is one of them, and out-of-compliance conditions increase risk.

Policy Variance Request Follow-Up

The Policy Administrator may need the help of other staff in Data Governance and of SMEs from the team that drafted the policy during the investigation.

The investigation should be carried out and a report should be prepared for the next meeting of the Data Policy Oversight Committee with recommendations. Ideally, the situation should be resolved with the organizational unit involved being able to provide a timeframe for operationalization.

These kinds of investigations should be highly unusual and are frankly inconvenient to all concerned. The worst-case scenario is that the organizational unit persistently refuses to operationalize the policy. At this point, the matter has to be referred to a higher authority than the Data Policy Oversight Committee, such as the Chief Risk Officer or Internal Audit. This escalation pathway is yet another point that has to be included in the policy of policies.

Closing Policy Variances

In the normal course of events, the organizational unit that has requested the variance will operationalize the policy and inform the Policy Administrator. The Policy

Administrator can then ask the Policy Registrar to close the variance in the Policy Request Log. Notes should be added to record the investigation and outcome. The Policy Administrator will also need to inform the Data Policy Oversight Committee. No action is required by the committee.

For variances that have been granted, the Policy Administrator must contact the organizational unit involved before the variance expires. Given that normal first-time variances usually last three months, this should be done about three weeks before expiration. The unit will have to submit a new request to extend the variance or operationalize the policy. Failure to do either will constitute a refusal to operationalize the policy, and the Data Policy Oversight Committee will invoke the escalation pathway discussed previously.

Figure 21.2 summarizes the overall process.

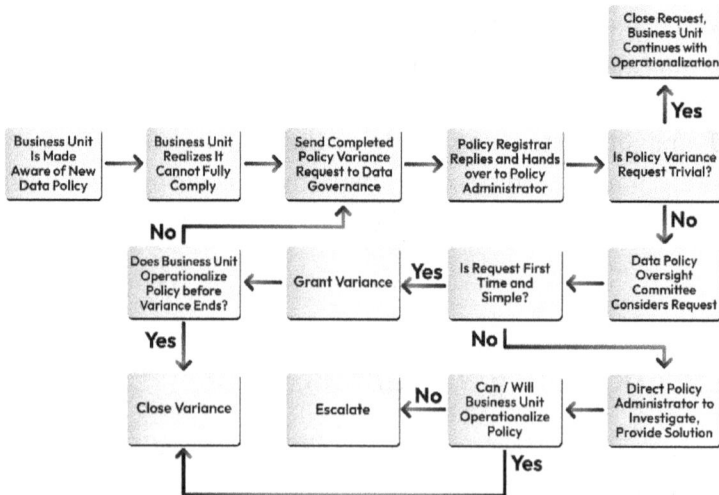

Figure 21.2: Summary of Policy Variance Process

Policy Impact of Variances

If a large number of variance requests are received for a given data policy, the Data Policy Oversight Committee must direct Data Governance to start an immediate review of the policy. An unusually high number of variance requests points to something being wrong with the policy. The review process will be the same as is normally carried out for each policy in the policy lifecycle, and we will discuss it in a subsequent chapter on policy reviews.

Coordination with Other Units

The policy variance process is conditionally permitting a noncompliance situation to persist. Other units such as Risk, Internal Audit, and Legal will need to know about it. The best way to achieve this is to have representation from these groups on the Data Policy Oversight Committee. They can then raise any objections to granting a variance and inform their respective groups of the situation so that they can adjust their activities. For instance, if Internal Audit is carrying out an audit, they should be aware of any variances granted or being considered for the area being examined.

If there are no members on the committee from an organizational unit that needs to be informed, then the Policy Administrator will need to carry out the coordination activities. It is best to avoid this extra work by having a broad enough representation on the Data Governance Oversight Committee.

Variance Metadata

Variances are captured in the Policy Request Log at a very basic level. The Policy Variance Request Form could be a simple online Word document that makes it easier for units to submit a variance request, but it is yet more policy metadata. As such, this information should also be operationalized in a metadata table. As discussed previously, it could be a spreadsheet, SaaS software, or configuration in a data catalog. This will also allow additional information to be captured for the variance, like Reason Codes for the request, which in turn can be used in reporting to analyze why there are variances and gain insights about improvements for data policies in general.

Planning for Variances

How variances will be handled must be included in the policy of policies. Details such as the exact procedure to follow and the variance request form are not part of the policy of policies, but their development should be mandated by the policy of policies. The procedure and the form should be well designed and well documented so it is easy for any organizational unit to follow the procedure and submit the form.

## Chapter 22

Data Policy Compliance Checking

C hecking compliance can begin after a policy has been promulgated and a reasonable time given for organizational units to operationalize it.

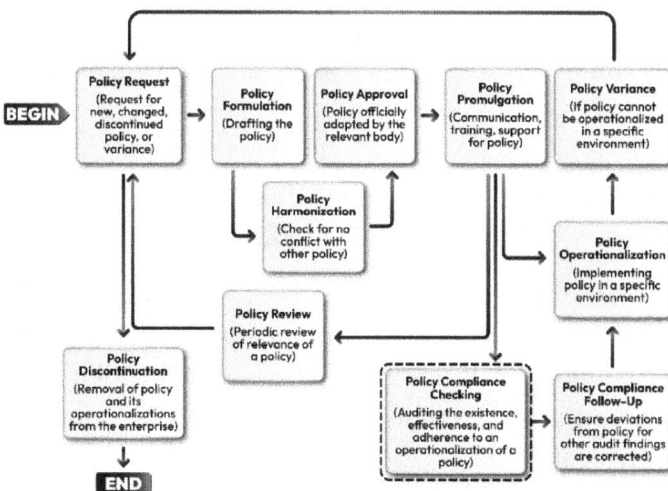

Figure 22.1: Policy Compliance Checking in the Policy Lifecycle

As mentioned earlier, a policy must be enforceable and enforced. A policy is not enforceable if compliance cannot be checked, perhaps because of resource or technical issues. And a policy is not enforced if compliance can be checked but nobody actually checks anything.

There are several major modalities for checking compliance that we will now discuss.

Attestation

Attestation is where an individual affirms that they are following a policy, including operationalizing it to the extent necessary in their business area. Usually, attestation is documented and the documentation preserved as proof of compliance.

It is acceptable for a Data Governance unit to manage attestation to data policies because Data Governance is not forming an opinion of compliance based on observation, but is simply compiling feedback from individuals who are not being influenced by Data Governance. Therefore, there is no issue about the separation of duties. Even so, this may not be appropriate for some highly regulated enterprises, and another unit will be tasked to gather the attestations.

Unfortunately, attestation is generally seen as a weak form of compliance checking. In many modern working environments, staff are fully occupied with their regular duties and are increasingly bombarded with information via email and messaging applications that take time to process and provide little value. A request for attestation will arrive amongst all this noise, and the simplest thing for a staff member to do is to attest that they are following the policy and there are no problems. It is this attitude that, in part, has raised questions about the general effectiveness of attestation.

Attestation Software

On the other hand, in some circumstances, attestation can be a beneficial approach. But before we can get to that, we need to discuss how to perform attestation.

> *In principle, attestation can be required of a large number of people in the enterprise, which means that simple manual processes will not scale.*

Furthermore, attestations must be documented. It is important to know who was requested to provide an attestation, who responded, who did not respond, and what additional information respondents provided.

Fortunately, there are a number of commercially available compliance software packages to use for attestation purposes. Data Governance should check with approval bodies and other organizational units that issue policies to determine if any of these packages are in use in the enterprise. There may well be an enterprise-level standard software package that can be used.

If Data Governance cannot find any attestation software, it may wish to acquire one. The tools very often have other capabilities too, such as in the area of Data Privacy. Requirements for these other capabilities may need to be included in the search for a tool. Of course, the process of acquisition and implementation can be lengthy, but acquiring a tool is a definite option.

Another option is to use a configurable SaaS workflow software tool to develop an attestation workflow. These tools are often very inexpensive and easy to use. The main thing to be careful of is to avoid the need to buy licenses for staff being asked to attest as users. This can dramatically increase the cost, and nobody likes to be given another tool they must learn.

Yet another option is to use online survey tools. These are plentiful and inexpensive. They provide request-response-like functionality, but without the workflow possibilities of the SaaS workflow tools. However, attestation does not always have to be complex, and so survey tools may be a fit. A drawback can be the lack of a database, meaning results must be downloaded and stored in another database to accumulate them for historical reporting and an audit trail.

If there is a corporate policy attestation tool, then Data Governance will need to use it and work with the administrators of the tool to prepare the attestation questions. An advantage of this situation is that attestation requests for all policies, not just data policies, can be sent out in a coordinated manner, which will likely be a more efficient way for staff to respond.

Attestation and Personally Oriented Policies

Some data policies are more oriented to individual responsibilities and behaviors, such as making sure data created by an individual is of high quality. Such policies apply to and are operationalized by individuals rather than organizational units. Therefore, attestation is a reasonable way to check compliance.

Typically, these attestations provide a link to the policy, and ask if the staff member has read and understands it. Some software solutions display the policy and there is a minimum time that is allowed for the staff to read it. How effective this technique actually is may be open to question, but again, it is a valid option.

Attestation at the Business Unit Level

Other data policies have to be operationalized at a business unit level. For these, the accountable person in each business unit has to be identified. If there is a well-formed Data Steward network in the enterprise, then Data Stewards can find out who the individuals are. Otherwise, the attestation requests will have to be sent to the head of the unit who can then forward them to the relevant individuals.

Business unit level attestations usually request more information than those at the personal level, such as:

- Level of operationalization of the policy. Perhaps the policy has been operationalized in part but not in whole.

- Description of how the policy has been operationalized.

- List of risks associated with the policy.

- Descriptions of how the risks have been mitigated.

- Any out of compliance conditions that have occurred and how they have been dealt with.

The more information that is requested, the greater the burden on Data Governance to process it. The information is useful for creating monitoring reports that show levels of compliance, but effort is required to produce them. Follow-up by Data Governance may also be needed if the attestation raises any questions about compliance. Such follow-up is necessary, but again requires effort.

Internal Audits

Organizational units like Internal Audit can also assess compliance as part of their routine examinations. They need to be fully prepared for carrying out their assessment activities.

We have already discussed special communications to Internal Audit during policy promulgation. Data Governance must ensure Internal Audit has a full understanding of the policy and answers any questions Internal Audit may have about how compliance can be assessed. Internal Audit will also want to know Data Governance's estimate of how long organizational units will take to comply. There is no point in assessing compliance until units in the enterprise have had a reasonable time to develop solutions. Of course, prior to this, Internal Audit can ask to see plans for compliance and assess them.

Where Internal Audit checks compliance with a data policy, there is less need for Data Governance to be involved in the compliance-checking process. Data Governance may still have to answer questions from Internal Audit to help understand the policy during an audit. If this happens, then Data Governance should note it for the next policy review as the policy may not be written clearly in some parts.

Data Governance should be informed by Internal Audit what audits were carried out and what the results were. Possibly, some of this information may need to be kept confidential, but there should be no problem with providing the overall counts. Monitoring reports can then be produced by Data Governance.

Data Governance should also find out where Internal Audit is reporting the results of its audits. Some industries are more heavily regulated than others, and Internal Audit may be reporting results to regulatory bodies. It is possible these regulatory bodies may come back to Data Governance with questions based on audit results, so it is important for Data Governance to be prepared.

External Auditors

The situation with external auditors is more or less the same as with Internal Audit. External auditors should be made aware of data policies and have the policies explained by Data Governance if the external auditors have data policies within their scope of compliance checking. Given that external auditors change over the years, Data Governance may have to provide such explanations periodically.

> A wrinkle with external auditors, and possibly with Internal Audit, is that they may wish to assess how Data Governance manages the policy lifecycle.

This can even involve attending meetings of the Data Policy Oversight Committee.

As mentioned, it is always possible to have a non-voting member from Internal Audit attend all committee meetings, which takes care of compliance assessment from their perspective. External auditors need to be made aware of the existence of the committee and provided with its schedule so they can decide if they want to attend. Satisfying external auditors is yet another reason for having a formal Data Policy Oversight Committee. If there is no committee and data policy management is done *ad hoc* by Data Governance, then there is a strong chance the external auditors would take issue. For enterprises in a regulated industry, this might escalate to the regulators being informed.

Data Surveillance

Data policies are about data, and data exists in data stores. As such, data can be inspected by automated tools. Those data policies related to data values and data structures rather than human behavior around data have the possibility of compliance checking being carried out by automated tools.

We can think of these tools as being data surveillance tools, and today they break down into three major classes:

- **Data Quality Tools.** These tools execute business rules provided by business users to check the validity of data values. They can also profile data automatically to find patterns of values in data and highlight outliers.

- **Data Classification Tools.** These tools examine data values and infer the category they belong to based on patterns known to the tools. For instance, they can recognize that a database column contains unencrypted US Social Security Numbers or the names of people.

- **Metadata Harvesting Tools.** These tools harvest metadata usually from database structures. E.g. they can be used to check if metadata like names of tables and columns conform to standards prescribed by policies.

If such tools exist in the enterprise, Data Governance may be able to use them to detect out of compliance conditions for certain data policies. However, Data Governance will need to discuss usage of the tools with the administrators, who are usually located in IT. A major issue is that these tools can use rather brute force approaches, like scanning entire databases, which can degrade the performance of these databases in terms of their normal processing functions. Additionally, if the tools and databases in question are Cloud-based, running these tools may result in very high costs being incurred with Cloud providers. Perhaps limited sampling methods may be sufficient for Data Governance's needs, which could get around these problems.

Data Governance can work closely with the groups that operate these tools to reuse their results for compliance checking. For instance, Information Security units often have Data Classification tools, and it is possible that the results from regular runs of these tools could be shared with Data Governance to determine if any out-of-compliance conditions can be detected with respect to data policies.

A more extreme approach is for Data Governance itself to acquire these tools and use them for compliance checking. However, once the question of technology to support data policies is raised, it typically leads in additional directions. Some data catalog tools offer support for data policies, and some of these data catalog tools have data quality and data classification capabilities. This takes us beyond the scope of data policies to the general metadata management needs of Data Governance and the federated metadata architecture that must exist to support these needs. Data policies are just one part of this puzzle, and although they are very important, they are a relatively small part. Data Governance needs an overall metadata strategy into which tools that support data policies will fit, but the scope involved is beyond what we can cover in this book.

Data Surveillance and Separation of Duties

If Data Governance does use data surveillance tools to detect out of compliance conditions with data policies, there may be a problem. This is because Data Governance acts like a legislature in creating data policies and an executive in enforcing them. Such a situation may be perfectly acceptable in many organizations, but not in others.

Where it is not acceptable, a unit other than Data Governance, such as IT Compliance, will need to operate the tools based on its understanding of the data policies. Obviously, Data Governance will need to work closely with such a unit.

> We do not yet see the emergence of specialized Data Compliance units whose task is to check compliance with data policies, but this could be a future development.

The current trend in most organizations appears to be that there is some tooling for data surveillance, and Data Governance directs its usage.

Whistleblowers

One additional way in which compliance can be checked is by allowing anyone in the enterprise to report noncompliance conditions that they have observed. Such individuals are usually termed "whistleblowers" in the USA.

There generally has to be a guarantee of anonymity and non-retaliation for whistleblowers to feel safe enough to report noncompliance. This, in turn, requires a general whistleblower policy to be in place, and usually a specific process for reporting noncompliance incidents. Data Governance is in no position to set this kind of thing up by itself. Either there will be an enterprise-level policy and process in place, or there will not. If there is, Data Governance should meet with the staff responsible so Data Governance can understand the process to deal with reported incidents of noncompliance with data policies. Data Governance may or may not be involved in the follow-up, depending on the enterprise.

Reporting about Compliance

We have reviewed a number of ways in which compliance can be checked. Different techniques may be more appropriate for particular policies, so a flexible approach is probably the best. The main issue is to ensure that any compliance checking done by Data Governance is as objective as possible. However, compliance reporting is also needed. A key component of the practice of data governance is proving that data is governed, which includes proving that compliance is being checked.

Reports that provide the results of compliance efforts prove that compliance is being checked and highlight any issues. Trends can be spotted over time, and metrics can be presented that show the state of compliance with data policies. The audience for these reports can be Data Governance internally, the Data Policy Oversight Committee, other areas of the business like Risk and Legal, and possibly regulators.

Therefore, Data Governance will need to develop the infrastructure to produce such reports, design them, and ensure they are distributed to the right parties after being put into production.

## Chapter 23

Policy Compliance Follow-Up

Ｏne or more out of compliance situations will inevitably be discovered for data policies.

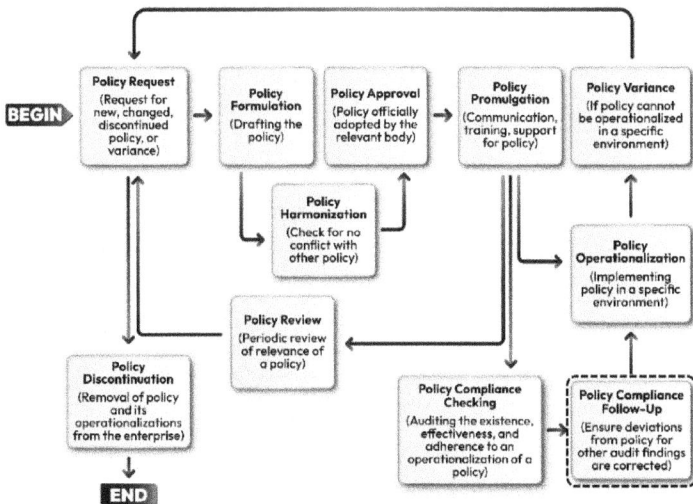

Figure 23.1: Policy Compliance Follow-up in the Policy Lifecycle

The question then arises as to what has to be done, but this depends on the circumstances.

Internal Audit Findings

If Internal Audit makes a "finding" during an audit of an organizational unit, there may be a standard process to "cure" the "finding." A "finding", in this context, is something that is out of compliance with a policy, which gets written up in the documentation of the audit. The problem has to be corrected or "cured."

While Internal Audit may have a standard process for curing a finding with a data policy, it does not have technical expertise, and it will almost certainly ask Data Governance to get involved. Once again, policy work is a two-edged sword for Data Governance. Policies require enterprise staff to do work to comply with them, but Data Governance also has to do a lot of work to support data policies.

Data Governance must be prepared, therefore, to assist with Internal Audit efforts to get audit findings cured. The organizational unit with the compliance issue will likely need to design a solution and have Data Governance agree that the design appears to be in compliance with the policy. Whether the design is adequately implemented is a different matter for Internal Audit to assess at a later date. Data Governance should not develop the solution, though it may explain how other organizational units have developed adequate solutions.

Data Governance should also be aware that Internal Audit often tracks the process of curing a finding, so whatever Data Governance puts in writing may enter into the corpus of documentation for the audit. Sometimes, specialized software tools are used for this purpose and Data Governance will have to use these tools for communications during the audit.

External Audit Findings

External audits tend to follow the same pattern as just described for Internal Audit. However, they typically also involve some enterprise unit that coordinates with the external auditors and will direct Data Governance about its involvement.

> *Very occasionally, external auditors may take issue with a data policy or the policy management processes used by Data Governance, which may occur if Data Governance itself gets audited.*

This is why it is so important to have fair, transparent, formal, robust, well-documented data policy management processes that can stand the scrutiny of an audit.

Findings by Regulators

Things can get worse in regulated industries, of which there are many today in developed countries. Regulators can carry out examinations (roughly the equivalent of audits). What might result from an examination is illustrated in the US banking sector, where a Matter Requiring Attention (MRA) can be raised. A MRA describes what has to be corrected and provides a timeframe for doing so. In practice, MRAs may be more nuanced, with a plan that satisfies the regulator being sufficient to resolve the MRA. However, the MRA may be reinstated if the plan is not delivered. Enterprises have to resist the temptation to develop an adequate plan and then relax and not implement it, only to find later that the MRA has come back.

Even worse is a MRIA, a Matter Requiring Immediate Attention. As the name suggests, this situation must be corrected immediately, and just creating a plan is not sufficient.

MRAs and MRIAs can be issued where defects in data policies are discovered, although regulators are not just looking at policies but trying to assess compliance with an entire regulatory framework. If Data Governance does get involved in a MRA for a data policy, they will find that a very senior manager or executive in the enterprise will be tasked with overseeing the corrective action. A formal project will likely be created, with an appropriate budget, to deal with the matter. External consultants may also be engaged. This is unlike the direct involvement by Data Governance in curing findings by Internal Audit, and Data Governance will most likely not be in a leading role.

Clearly, this kind of situation is politically sensitive, so Data Governance must be alert to ensure that it fully participates in the project and delivers whatever it commits to on time with the required quality.

The only situation that is even worse than MRAs and MRIAs is where there is a settlement, or "consent order," with the regulators over criminal or civil charges brought by the regulators or judicial authorities against an enterprise. The result will probably be a whole program of projects, and may require strengthening data policies, as a failure of this magnitude likely involved data, and the data policies were not sufficient to prevent it.

Reactions to Compliance Issues with Data Policies

Data Governance should document every compliance issue with data policies that comes to light and how the issue was addressed. This documentation is important for auditors and regulators, but it is also important for Data Governance to help identify and address gaps in how data policies are being managed and implemented.

Data Governance must find out the root cause of any instance of noncompliance.

Remember that organizational units have the option to request a policy variance if they cannot immediately comply with a policy.

So, an organizational unit that is out of compliance with a data policy has either not bothered to request a variance or has not adequately operationalized the policy.

Data Governance needs to determine if something went wrong with the policy. Perhaps there were problems such as:

- Was the policy promulgation phase inadequate?

- Was the policy poorly written, such that the organizational unit involved misinterpreted it, or thought it did not apply to them?

- Was the policy such that it could not be adequately operationalized in the context of the organizational unit involved, even though they tried?

Such situations would indicate that there is an issue with the policy itself, or the policy management processes. Data Governance needs to be very sensitive to these possibilities whenever an out-of-compliance condition occurs.

There could be an internal investigation process in Data Governance, driven by the Data Policy Operations Committee, after every out-of-compliance condition has been successfully addressed to determine root causes. The results could be presented to the Data Governance Oversight Committee. Getting the conclusions about out-of-compliance conditions into the minutes of the committee will also help Data Governance preserve a useful audit trail of how it addressed these conditions.

Chapter 24

Data Policy Review

Policies must be living documents. They exist in the context of an enterprise that itself exists in ever-changing economic, social, competitive, technology, and regulatory conditions.

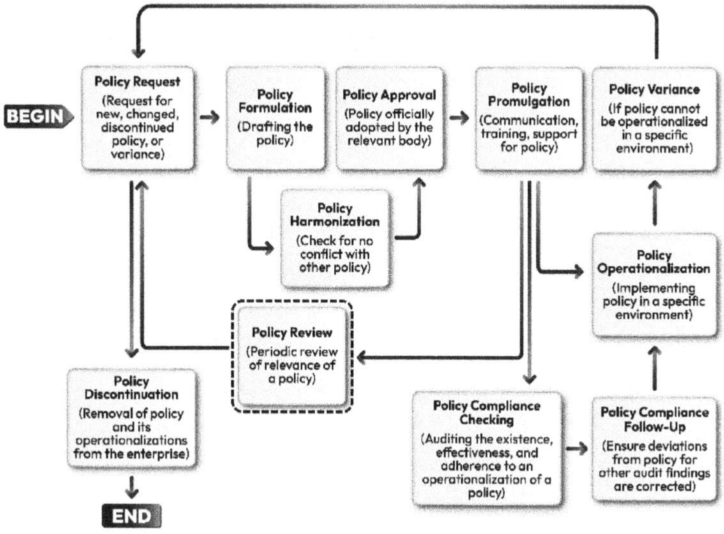

Figure 24.1: Policy Review in the Policy Lifecycle

As a result, there is no guarantee that a data policy will remain static in its original drafted form.

Scheduling Reviews

Review every data policy at least annually. The Policy Administrator who manages the policy is responsible for getting this done. Since there will be a number of data policies, it is easier to carry out the review in a way that is evenly paced throughout the year. This will optimize the level of Data Governance resources that can be allocated for each review and prevent a set of reviews that happen all at the same time, overwhelming the normal work of Data Governance.

When a policy is promulgated, the date of the first review should be set. It should happen no earlier than 4 months and no later than 12 months after promulgation in the month with the least number of policy reviews yet scheduled. Thereafter, it can occur every 12 months from this date.

The scheduling should be done in a Data Governance Social Calendar where all future administrative events are scheduled, not just those connected with policies. This calendar must be visible to all staff in Data Governance. The Policy Administrator is responsible for updating the calendar to schedule the policy reviews.

It may be thought that a workflow for each policy could trigger a reminder for the policy review. However, this is not advisable because Data Governance needs to see the totality of its scheduled obligations at a glance.

This means that all future events have to be scheduled in one place, not as an array of individual workflows that would have to be examined one by one to see what is happening in the future.

The Data Governance Social Calendar is the best option.

The Policy Administrator should set up the calendar to send automatic reminders during each of the 3 weeks prior to the scheduled policy review to all who will participate. This should be sufficient notice for people to clear their calendars.

Metadata Requirements for Policy Reviews

There are two major metadata needs to support policy reviews:

- **A Policy Review Report.** This is a report that is created for every policy review. It has a standard template that needs to be designed by the Data Policy Operations Committee. A report is completed for every policy review. The standard format helps ensure reviews are carried out in a similar way by all Policy Administrators and nothing that is required is forgotten.

- **A Policy Review Log.** This is yet another simple list. It has one record for each policy review that is performed. The name of the policy, the dates the review began and ended, the outcome of the review, the names of the participants, and a link to the Policy Review Report should all be included. As with similar lists, a data catalog, a SaaS database product, or even an Excel spreadsheet can be used to support the log.

Obviously, different enterprises will have their own specific requirements for each of these metadata items. The policy should include a provision to make sure they are developed.

Uniform Review Procedure

> *Data policy reviews must be done the same way for all policies. It cannot be that each Policy Administrator does a review in whatever way they feel like.*

The best way to achieve uniformity that promotes fairness and transparency in data policy reviews is for Data Governance to collectively design a procedure that can then be executed for each policy review.

Table 24.1 provides an example of such a procedure.

#	Step Description
1	Policy Administrator gathers all support requests for the policy received since the previous review.
2	Policy Administrator gathers documents relating to all out-of-compliance incidents reported since the last scheduled review.
3	Policy Administrator prepares the Policy Review Report from the support requests and compliance incidents. If there have been none, the report simply states this.
4	Policy Administrator sends an email naming the data policy and stating that it needs to be reviewed and attaching the Policy Review Report. The email asks recipients to provide any reasons why the policy should be updated. The email is sent to: • The Head of Data Governance • The experts in the working group who drafted the policy • The stakeholders who were consulted at the time of policy formulation • The individuals who made the support requests • The individuals involved in the compliance incidents • To the heads of units that are Data Governance partners, like Legal or Risk.
5	The Policy Administrator ensures that each recipient of the email provides a response, unless there is a valid reason they cannot.
6	The Policy Administrator updates the Policy Review Report with the names of the email recipients and their responses.
7	If there have been no suggestions to update the policy, the Policy Administrator adds this to the Policy Review Report.
8	If there are any suggestions for updating the policy, the Policy Administrator convenes a meeting with all the experts who drafted the policy, plus anyone else who suggested an update.

#	Step Description
9	The meeting reviews the suggested updates. Possible outcomes are: • If the group decides no updates are needed, then the policy is left unchanged. • If the group decides that non-material changes are needed, such as spelling or punctuation, then the policy will be updated. • If the group decides that material changes are required, then the Policy Administrator is authorized to submit a policy request for the update.
10	The Policy Administrator updates the Policy Review Report with the group's decision, circulates it to all members, and files it in the policy document store.
11	If non-material changes are required, the Policy Administrator updates a copy of the policy and circulates it to all members of the group. Unless any member objects within two working weeks, the changes are considered finalized.
12	If no updates are needed, then the Policy Administrator updates the Last Reviewed Date of the official version of the policy to the date when the group's decision was made.
13	If non-material updates are needed, then the Policy Administrator updates the official version of the policy with the changes and sets the Last Reviewed Date to the date when the group's decision was made.
14	If material changes are needed, the Policy Administrator sends a formal policy request for the changes to the Policy Registrar along with the report.
15	The Policy Administrator finalizes the Policy Review Report and emails all the individuals listed in (4) above to inform them that the review is over, what the results of the review are, and a link to the Policy Review Report.

Table 24.1: Example of Policy Review Procedure

Simple Policy Changes

It is likely that a data policy review will not lead to any changes in most cases. All that happens then is that the official version of the policy, which is accessible via the intranet as a document, is updated with a new Last Reviewed Date. As previously discussed, this date assures readers that the policy is a living document that is being kept up to date. In such cases, the Policy Review Report will be very short and simply show that the review process was carried out.

Non-material changes in the policy are likely to be for spelling and grammar. These should have been caught during the formulation phase, so if they keep getting found in the review phase, they may indicate a larger problem.

Some non-material changes may be related to information in the policy about dates, names of people, names of organizational units, physical locations, email addresses, and intranet links. We have previously discussed the need to keep as much "hard-coding" of this kind of information as possible out of policies. However, there always has to be some. Perhaps the Data Governance unit has its name changed from "Data Management" to "Enterprise Data Governance." Perhaps there is a major reorganization of the entire intranet of the enterprise and the links to data policies are now on a different page.

Since the substance of the policy is not changing with these kinds of non-material changes, there is no need to create a policy request to go through the policy lifecycle. The Policy Administrator simply has to update the official version of the policy with the new information. The Policy Review

Report must also describe these changes and record the fact that they were considered to be non-material.

Where things get tricky is the boundary between non-material and material changes. For instance, suppose the policy statements have to be reordered in a data policy. You could argue that the substance of the policy has not changed, but the policy will now look quite different to enterprise staff.

> *Because data policies have a widespread impact on the enterprise, the temptation to reduce administrative effort in their management must be resisted.*

We can only do direct updates to policies without creating a policy request when there will be minimal impact on the reader. Anything else requires the additional effort of going through the policy lifecycle.

One other important item to note is that having only one official copy of a data policy makes the update process much easier. Having multiple copies greatly increases the work needed and the risk that one copy may be overlooked and not updated.

Material Changes to a Policy

A material change to a policy requires the Policy Administrator to submit a policy request to the Policy Registrar. The policy request for an update to a policy needs to be considered by the Data Policy Oversight Committee as soon as possible, as the old version of the policy is still the official version, but there is clearly a need for a change. There may be a risk exposure while this situation persists. The Policy Review Report should be sent to the committee as part of the policy request.

When it meets to consider the policy request, the committee should be in a position to be fully informed. After all, the Policy Administrator will have met with the members of the original working group. Their advice will have been captured in the Policy Review Report provided to the committee. Ideally, the Policy Review Report will contain the changes that are required for the policy, but this may not always be possible.

However, there may be issues. Perhaps none of the experts who served on the original working group were available to be consulted. Perhaps the material changes that are required could not be recommended in the Policy Review Report because they arise from changed circumstances, like business strategy or new regulations, that members of the original working group are unfamiliar with. Under these conditions, the committee will likely need to direct the formation of a new working group and recommend experts for it.

At this point, the same procedure will be followed for policy formulation, except that a new version of the policy is being formulated rather than a completely new policy.

Alternatively, if the committee considers that the Policy Review Report contains a complete and acceptable proposal for an updated version of the policy, then no working group is needed to formulate anything, and the Policy Administrator can send the draft new version of the policy to the policy harmonization step in the policy lifecycle.

New Policy Version and Policy Bulletin

If the policy review results in a new version of the policy, then the Policy Administrator will need to change the Version Number in the header of the official policy document at the point the new version is released, which contains all the updates.

Concurrently with the update of the policy document, the Policy Bulletin must be issued with a description of the changes in the new version. Staff in the enterprise will expect to see a summary of what changed and that the policy document has changed in synch with the release of the Policy Bulletin. If these two are not aligned, it looks terrible, so the logistics to keep them aligned are necessary, even if they require considerable effort. Perhaps updating the policy and scheduling the Policy Bulletin last thing on a Friday for release first thing on the following Monday can be a useful tactic.

Higher Level Process Reviews

Policy review is not always concerned with a specific data policy. It is an opportunity to learn lessons about data policies in general and share them with everyone in the Data Governance unit who has a role or interest in data policies.

The Data Policy Operations Committee is the appropriate venue to do this. Lessons learned about a specific data policy can be shared among the participants. However, the committee also needs to periodically undertake an even higher form of review, which is linked with evaluation.

The Data Policy Operations Committee must be responsible for optimizing the data policy management processes and any supporting software. Process optimization is required for what is known as Level 5 in the Capability Maturity Modem Integration (CMMI). This is a framework that was originally designed to identify high-quality software development practices, but it has since become more generally applied. Level 5 is the highest level that can be attained. It signifies that processes are being measured and that a mechanism is in place to optimize them over time. While not all capabilities need to be at Level 5, data policies are so important that the capability to optimize data policy management processes needs to exist. The Data Policy Operations Committee fulfills this requirement. Process optimization first requires evaluation to be performed on the processes. See Table 24.2 for a summary of the CMMI levels.

Level	Level Label	Level Summary	Level Description
5	Optimizing	Stable and flexible	Organization is focused on continuous improvement and is built to pivot and respond to opportunity and change. The organization's stability provides a platform for agility and innovation.

Level	Level Label	Level Summary	Level Description
4	Quantitatively Managed	Measured and controlled	Organization is data-driven with quantitative performance improvement objectives that are predictable and aligned to meet the needs of internal and external stakeholders.
3	Defined	Proactive, rather than reactive	Organization-wide standards provide guidance across projects, programs, and portfolios.
2	Managed	Managed on the project level	Projects are planned, performed, measured, and controlled.
1	Initial	Unpredictable and reactive	Work gets completed but is often delayed and over budget.
0	Incomplete	Ad hoc and unknown.	Work may or may not get completed.

Table 24.2: Summary of Capability Maturity Modem Integration (CMMI) Levels

(adapted from https://cmmiinstitute.com/learning/appraisals/levels)

Monitoring is distinct from evaluation and involves dealing with any immediate issues that are general in nature in terms of data policy processes and any supporting software. Evaluation involves examining long-term trends to try to confirm that everything is working as it should, finding opportunities for improvement, discovering and mitigating risks, and predicting possible future issues. It is from the evaluation activities that recommendations for process improvements come.

The Data Policy Operations Committee should take the opportunity of policy reviews to evaluate the policy administration processes. At least annually, it should report to the Data Policy Oversight Committee on the health of these processes and the need for any changes. All changes have to be approved by the Data Policy Oversight Committee.

Sometimes, recommendations for change may be needed outside of this annual cycle. Occasionally, the Data Policy Oversight Committee itself may recognize the need for a policy process change and direct the Data Policy Operations Committee to implement it.

All of these policy management requirements connected with policy reviews have to be factored into the policy of policies when it is being developed.

## Chapter 25

Data Policy Discontinuation

Few policies are destined to exist forever. For example, decades ago, mainframe computers were programmed using punched cards, but today, punched cards have entirely disappeared. And the policies that were needed to manage punched cards (which could be quite complex) have also disappeared.

While this is easy to understand, we also have the situation of policy reviews, which can lead to the update of a policy as a new version. It may be possible for a policy to just keep evolving forever with each review. Eventually, there is a new version that is totally different to the initial version. But is a policy that is utterly different from its initial version really the same policy? What these considerations point to is that there must be criteria to determine when a policy must be discontinued, and whether it is replaced by a new policy or not replaced at all.

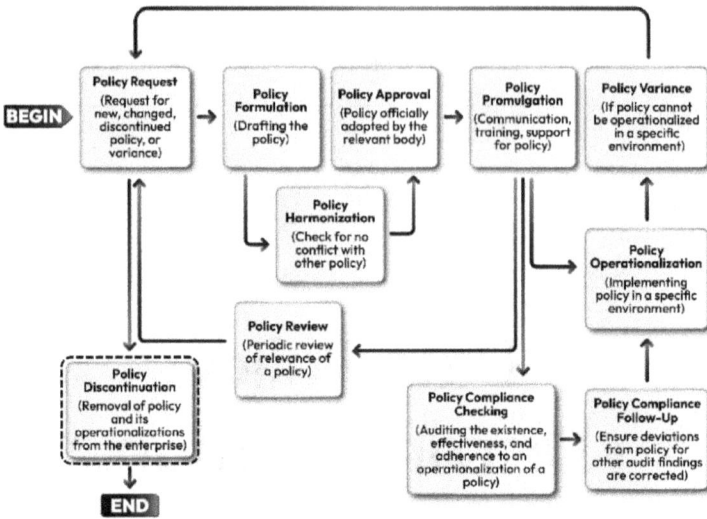

Figure 25.1: Policy Discontinuation in the Policy Lifecycle

Policy Discontinuation Criteria

While policy discontinuation will always be a rare event, we propose the following criteria to determine when it should happen:

- **The rationale for the policy no longer exists.** This is what happened in the case of punched cards.

- **The title of the policy has to change.** If the content of the policy has evolved to a point where the title of the policy no longer describes it, then the policy should be discontinued and replaced by another.

- **The policy content has changed by 15% or more since the initial version.** In this case, the policy content has evolved to be more than 15% different from the initial version. Staff who had to operationalize the initial version will have to make significant updates to their processes with a change of this magnitude. They will probably think of the situation as one where the previous processes had to be replaced by new processes. It is simply less confusing to discontinue the old policy and issue a new one. This happened when the European Union introduced the General Data Protection Regulation (GDPR). Many enterprises had Data Privacy policies based on the prior legal framework, which the GDPR replaced. These policies likewise had to be replaced.

Perhaps some enterprises can have different criteria. The point is that the decision to discontinue a policy cannot be taken in an *ad hoc* manner. Instead, a uniform approach must be applied.

The need to have explicit criteria for discontinuing a policy can be incorporated into the policy of policies. The policy of policies does not have to specify what the criteria are, but direct that they are developed.

Policy Review and Discontinuation

The decision to discontinue a policy must come about as a result of applying the discontinuation criteria during a policy review. This means that the criteria must be applied during every policy review. Probably in nearly every review, it will be found that the criteria do not apply, but the check should be made and documented.

If it is found that a policy should be discontinued, then a policy request must be generated and sent to the Policy Registrar. If a new policy has to be formulated to replace the discontinued one, then it is probably easier to add this to the policy request rather than generate yet another policy request.

If a new policy is required, the procedures can follow the policy lifecycle from policy formulation onwards.

Approval of Discontinuation

The Data Policy Oversight Committee will have to approve the policy request for the discontinuation. When it does so, it must set the date on which the policy will no longer apply. This should allow a reasonable time for promulgation and for organizational units to prepare for the discontinuation.

There is no need for the policy harmonization step in terms of a discontinued policy, as there is nothing to harmonize. Therefore, the policy request can proceed to the policy approval step for the discontinuation.

Promulgation of a Discontinuation

Once all approvals have been obtained, it is time to promulgate the discontinuation.

Since a policy discontinuation is a major event, it requires a great deal of communication.

It may be necessary to communicate the fact that there is an intent to discontinue the policy well in advance.

The promulgation includes the use of the Policy Bulletin, which can contain an item every month tracking the progress of the policy request for discontinuation. Initially, the Policy Bulletin should ask staff to plan for the discontinuation but take no action until the discontinuation is fully approved and the discontinuation date is set. Promulgation via other channels can also be considered, such as direct emails to or meetings with groups known to have operationalized the policy.

Once the discontinuation has been fully approved, the communications can be more specific, providing the date when the discontinuation will occur. Units within the enterprise will need to decide for themselves if they need to remove any procedures they have put in place previously to comply with the policy. This may well be needed if the policy is replaced by another.

Operationalization of Discontinuation

On the date the policy is discontinued, the official copy of the policy should be marked prominently as being discontinued. It can still be left in place at this point since staff may search for it and become confused if they cannot find it. Eventually, the policy will have to be removed. This may be a standard period, such as three months after discontinuation, which can be specified in the policy of policies.

Not only will the policy have to be removed, but all links to it will also have to be removed.

It may be difficult to find all the links that lead to the policy, so the policy can be replaced with a document that indicates the policy has been removed or simply links to a page with information about discontinued policies.

All the compliance measures for the policy will also have to be discontinued at this point. Internal Audit should be aware of the discontinuation long before it happens. Data surveillance tools should be reconfigured to remove compliance checking for the policy. Requests for attestation should be removed.

As can be understood, many actions are involved in discontinuing a policy, and given that it will happen rarely, it is a good idea to develop a checklist of everything that must be done so that nothing is forgotten.

End of the Policy Lifecycle

At this point, we have come to the end of the policy lifecycle which we have traced from the request for a new policy all the way through to the discontinuation of the policy. It is the efficient but thorough management of the policy lifecycle that guarantees successful and sustainable data policies

Chapter 26

Conclusion

There is much more about data policies than in this book, particularly about the subject matter of these policies. We have attempted to describe a framework for ensuring that data policies are successful and sustainable. A well-written data policy alone will not produce any successful or sustainable outcome—a robust institutional machine is needed for that.

The benefits that can be realized from data policies are enormous. In the long run, attitudes to data can be reshaped across an enterprise. Because data policies focus on practical human behavior concerning data, they are much more consumable than initiatives that emphasize technologies for data management and initiatives that involve more general, theoretical constructs about data.

Nearly all staff in nearly all enterprises are predisposed to take policies seriously. As a result, they will take data policies seriously, which is a huge advantage for the mission of Data Governance. However, it does mean that data policies must be of the highest quality, be seen as the products of a transparent and well-organized set of processes, and be robustly supported.

In other words, policies provide Data Governance with a very effective tool but demand the very best performance from Data Governance.

That is why this book places so much emphasis on the institutionalization of data policies.

Since data policies exist for the long run in a steady state, they also have an advantage over point-in-time organizational change management projects that seek to build a data culture or promote data literacy. Such projects are still worthwhile, but their effects can fade with time, whereas data policies are always present and complied with.

The long-term effects of data policies will be even more valuable in the future as the role of data expands. Traditionally, "data" has meant the structured data found in relational databases produced as a result of the operational processes of an enterprise. That is now shifting to include unstructured data, such as pure text, images, audio, and video content, which is needed for AI. There is also an increasing interest in sensor data from control systems that are found in robots, cars, aircraft, and so on. Data about human attitudes and behaviors, especially in the areas of economics and financial markets, is already an industry in its own right and is expanding rapidly. Not only is the supply side of data growing, but so is the demand side, with AI's voracious appetite for data.

What this means is that the scope of data policies will need to grow in the future to deal with all these new requirements. In an earlier chapter, we briefly discussed policy gap analysis in the context of current states. Going forward, Data Governance must be more aligned with business and technical strategy to anticipate the need for completely new data policies. The alternative is for rapid organic growth to occur, which will almost certainly result in creating a new "data mess" and belated data policies that may not fully stabilize and control the situation.

Yet, in a very real sense, the future has never looked brighter for data policies. The need for data policies will only increase because of these new technologies, business, and data developments. This is not to stifle the implementation of new strategies, although risk reduction will always be very important. Rather, it is to promote the very best data governance and management practices that will increase the efficiency and effectiveness of implementing these strategies. It is now up to Data Governance to seize the initiative and play a leading role as this new world unfolds.

Glossary of Terms

Specialized terms used in this book are defined in the table below.

Term	Definition
Business Glossary	A list of terms, their definitions, and other metadata managed in a data catalog.
Capability Maturity Model Integration (CMMI)	An industry standard set of levels that describe the maturity of a software development process.
Cloud Computing	An infrastructure where computing resources are reached via the Internet.
Compliance	The condition of practices being carried out in accordance with policies.
Critical Success Factor	Something that has to be in place for the goals to be attained.
Data Acquisition	The process of bringing datasets into a data lake, often from outside the enterprise.
Data Classification Tool	A software product that can categorize a data element based on its values in the context in which they are found.
Data Dictionary	A list of the tables and columns in a database or file, with supporting information like technical characteristics and definitions.
Data Directive	Anything approved by the enterprise that tells staff what data management to do, or how to do manage data.

Term	Definition
Data Governance	(a) The decision-making framework that determines how data will be managed in an enterprise; (b) the organizational unit responsible for operating the decision-making framework.
Data Governance Partners	Enterprise units that have capabilities Data Governance requires to carry out its work.
Data Lake	A database environment that stores datasets until they are needed for use, and supports the processing of these datasets when usage is known.
Data Literacy	The education of staff in an enterprise to be able to better understand data concepts and so be positioned to better undertake data management.
Data Management	The set of processes needed to ensure the enterprise data resource is available, usable, can be trusted, and is fully compliant with all legal and policy requirements.
Data Model	A design blueprint for a database.
Data Pipelines	A series of steps to move and transform data from an initial form to a final form that matches a requirement.
Data Policy Operations Committee	A committee located within a Data Governance unit that is responsible for the general management tasks required for data policies.
Data Policy Oversight Committee	A committee that ensures data policies are of high quality and being managed in accordance with established procedures and standards.

Term	Definition
Data Quality	The practice of ensuring data is free of defects and can be used for its intended purposes.
Data Quality Tool	A software product that can detect actual or possible data quality defects.
Data Warehouse	A database environment that integrates and processes pre-existing production data to reshape it for certain kinds of queries.
Database	An environment that manages related datasets.
Datacenter	A physical installation where computer hardware is housed.
Dataset	A unit of structured data that can be managed as a whole, for example, a file.
Enterprise Policy Site	A single intranet site that an enterprise has established to house information about all policies in the enterprise.
Goal	An outcome, usually in the long term, that supports a vision and/or mission.
Master Data Management	The specialized management of data pertaining to the things that participate in the transaction of an enterprise.
Memorandum of Understanding	A written document specifying how two organizational units will work together.
Metadata	The information needed to understand and manage the information assets of the enterprise.
Mission	How we get to the ideal state.
Objective	Something measurable, usually an output of an activity, that helps to achieve a goal.

Term	Definition
Operating Model	A set of organizational bodies and their interrelationships, usually in the context of a particular strategy.
Operational System	A system that processes the transactions of an enterprise.
Organizational Change Management OCM	A strategic approach to changing something major in an enterprise, such as culture or parts of the business model.
Policy Compliance Follow-Up	This occurs if there is a compliance "finding," that is, an out-of-compliance situation for a particular policy. It is expected that the Data Governance unit will help the business unit that is out of compliance to take action to get into compliance. This is because the Data Governance unit is best placed to explain the policy in detail.
Policy	A high-level imperative that controls business behavior. It supports one or more principles. A policy specifies what to do, but not how to do it. A policy is enforceable and enforced.
Policy Administrator	An individual tasked with managing a data policy across all phases in the policy lifecycle.
Policy Approval	The new or updated draft policy goes to any organizational body that is required to approve policies. There may be multiple such bodies. They also have to approve policy discontinuations.

Term	Definition
Policy Bulletin	An accumulating list of all data policy actions so that anyone in the enterprise can see information about new, changed, or discontinued data policies.
Policy Compliance Checking	Someone has to be responsible for checking that the policy is complied with, and they must perform the checks. There can be all kinds of ways of doing this, and automation may be possible for certain data policies.
Policy Coordination	The cooperation between two policy-setting units so each is aware of the other's policy work.
Policy Discontinuation	If a policy is no longer relevant or simply does not work, it must be discontinued. The policy may be replaced by another policy.
Policy Formulation	The development of a new policy, with controls and checks in the drafting process.
Policy Harmonization	The checking that a new or changed policy does not conflict with any other policy. All enterprise policies should be checked, not just data policies. Any conflicts have to be resolved.
Policy Lifecycle	The set of distinct management activities that must be carried out on a policy from its inception until it is no longer needed.
Policy of Policies	A policy that specifies how data policies are to be governed and managed.

Term	Definition
Policy Operationalization	It is up to individuals, business units, and teams impacted by the policy to put it into practice. Sometimes what has to be done is obvious, but sometimes it is not. Operationalization may vary from context to context.
Policy Promulgation	Informing the enterprise about the new, changed, or discontinued policy. This is a communications effort primarily, but sometimes training may be needed for a policy. Support for the policy is also provided.
Policy Registrar	An individual tasked with keeping the portfolio of data policies up to date, and handling all policy requests.
Policy Request	Policy work starts with a formal request of some kind. Very often this is a decision within the Data Governance unit, or equivalent, that is responsible for data policies, but sometimes requests can come from outside this unit. Requests do not have to be for a new policy. They might be to change or discontinue a policy.
Policy Review	All policies need to be periodically reviewed to ensure they are up to date with business, regulatory, technology, and other realities. If it is felt that a policy needs to be updated or discontinued, a policy request is raised, and the lifecycle begins all over again. In addition to policies, the procedures and organizational structures for governing and managing data policies are also reviewed.

Term	Definition
Policy Statement	An atomic instruction in a policy.
Policy Style Guide	The set of standards for writing text in a data policy.
Policy Variance	If an individual or business unit cannot operationalize part or all of a policy, they can request to be exempted from it for a specific period of time.
Practice	A way to implement a policy and/or achieve an objective.
Principle	A statement of fundamental belief that cannot be further analyzed and must be accepted as true or false.
Procedure	A set of instructions for performing a task in a logical sequence.
RACI matrix	A technique for establishing role clarity across a set of tasks based on four types of role: Responsible; Accountable; Consulted; Informed.
Repository	A database that stores metadata.
Semantic Model	In the context of data lakes, a storage model that is based on the understanding of a dataset, the creation of a data model for the dataset, and the physical implementation of this data model.
Stakeholder	An individual whose work is affected by something, such as a data policy.
Standard	A practice that is mandated.
Storage Model	An architecture for the storage of datasets without having to design a data model for them.
Strategy	A plan that is broad in scope (perhaps enterprise-wide), longer term, and intended to help achieve the vision.

Term	Definition
Structured Data	Data that is organized into rows and columns.
Structured Metadata	Metadata that is organized into rows and columns.
Subject Matter Expert (SME)	An individual recognized for knowledge or skill in a particular area.
Success Criteria	The specific measures by which attaining an objective is assessed.
Tactic	A plan for a single step or task or some other part of a Strategic Plan.
Unstructured Data	Data that is not organized into rows and columns. Examples include documents, images, audio, and video.
Unstructured Metadata	Metadata that is not organized into rows and columns. Examples include documents, images, audio, and video.
Vision	A description of the ideal state.

Index

www.ingramcontent.com/pod-product-compliance
Lightning Source LLC
Chambersburg PA
CBHW071542210326

41597CB00019B/3082